To Pat — ✓ with the compliments of a. Pierce Middleton + Sept. 19, 1996

NEW WINE IN OLD SKINS

Liturgical Change and the Setting of Worship

Arthur Pierce Middleton

Illustrations by Charles Dickinson

MOREHOUSE-BARLOW
Wilton, Connecticut

Morehouse-Barlow Co. Inc.
78 Danbury Road
Wilton, Connecticut 06897

Library of Congress Cataloging-in-Publication Data

Middleton, Arthur Pierce.
  New wine in old skins.

  Bibliography: p.
  Includes index.
  1. Liturgy and architecture. 2. Church decoration
and ornament. I. Title.
NA4605.M54   1988   246′.9583   88-8908
ISBN 0-8192-1432-9

Printed in the United States of America
by
BSC LITHO, Harrisburg, PA

Dedicated to

Marion J. Hatchett
priest, liturgiologist, and facilitator of
Prayer Book revision

and

Sherrill Scales, Jr.
priest, architect, and facilitator of
new and retrofitted church buildings

Contents

Observations from the past

All things flow; nothing abides.
Heraclitus (c. 535–475 B.C.)

Times change, and we change with them.
Latin proverb

The more things change, the more they stay the same.
French proverb

Change is not made without inconvenience, even from worse to better.
Richard Hooker (1554–1600)

Here below to live is to change, and to be perfect is to have changed much.
John Henry Newman (1801–1890)

About the Author

Educated in medieval and British history at Edinburgh University and holding a Ph.D. in early American history from Harvard, Canon Middleton was lecturer in colonial history at the College of William & Mary (1946-1948) and director of research for Colonial Williamsburg (1948-1954). After taking priest's orders, he served parishes in Southern Virginia, Connecticut, and Western Massachusetts, was rural dean of South Berkshire, historiographer of the diocese of Western Massachusetts, and canon of Christ Church Cathedral, Springfield, MA. He was also editor of THE ANGLICAN, 1954-1980, author of AMIABLE DWELLINGS: THE EPISCOPAL CHURCHES OF WESTERN MASSA-CHUSETTS (1976), and a reader/consultant to the Standing Liturgical Commission during the recent Prayer Book revision. Upon retiring in 1980 he returned to his native Maryland and has served as a trustee of the Episcopal Church Building Fund and field consultant of the Episcopal Commission on Religious Art and Architecture.

To the Reader: A Study in Change

This book is about change, over many years, in the liturgical action of the Church and, therefore, in the architectural setting of worship. It contains little that is new. What is novel about it is that it is an assemblage of generally accepted facts that have not been put together before. It is not intended for scholars who already know its contents but for parish priests, church architects, and other interested persons who face the need to rearrange church interiors to accommodate current liturgical practice.

It is not a "how-to-do-it" book. The wide variety of church interiors precludes the possibility of one book laying down specifically the way all should be rearranged. After all, the Victorian Ecclesiologists did just that, and, thanks to their success, they wrought havoc in almost every church built before 1840! A more pragmatic way is to sketch the historical background and then deal with each church on its own merits, taking into account spatial considerations, available funds, and the extent to which priest and people are prepared to make changes. My intention is to provide information relating both to past changes and to interior arrangements that are necessary or implied by the rubrics of the 1979 *Book of Common Prayer*. With that as a background, each parish with the help of an architect can develop plans for retrofitting with some degree of confidence.

In my experience, many people are anxious to improve their setting of worship but are fearful (and rightly so) of doing violence to old churches and to Anglican tradition. Several of the sections of this book that deal with such things as altars, pulpits, and sedilia were originally written as reports to parishes in answer to specific questions. The general unfamiliarity with the past, in these matters, often renders otherwise well-informed persons unable to distinguish between ancient and recent practices or between permanent and transient ones and therefore makes them needlessly uneasy about

1

exchanging a practice that was a novelty in their grandparents' day for one that can claim a thousand years of Christian use. The role of this book is, therefore, to acquaint the reader with the gradual but kaleidoscopic changes that have taken place over the centuries and to demonstrate the fact that in rearranging the architectural setting of worship to meet current liturgical practice a parish will be in the mainstream of Christian history, acting as most parishes have done in the past nineteen centuries. If, on the other hand, a parish chooses to cling to an outmoded setting, it invites trouble. On the basis of experience I can predict that it may impede conformity to current liturgical practice and either isolate itself from the Church at large or undermine confidence in the adequacy of the existing parish church to meet the needs of the Prayer Book and the ceremonial that elsewhere accompanies it.

Because of its modest intent, I have not weighted the pages of this book with footnotes containing elaborate documentation. Instead, for the benefit of the reader whose interest is piqued, I have provided a bibliography that should afford sufficient reading matter for many a day.

How This Book Came To Be Written

In the course of serving as a field consultant for the Episcopal Church Building Fund, visiting parishes from Massachusetts to Georgia, and by means of correspondence elsewhere as well, I have come to realize that few people have any idea how liturgy— especially ceremonial—has undergone substantial change over the centuries and that these modifications have resulted in considerable changes in the physical setting of worship. Indeed, changing ways of worship almost inevitably require some rearrangement of church interiors. If the necessary retrofitting is left undone, the worshiping community will eventually decide that the old church is no longer suitable and will cast about for means to build a new church. And if they succeed, it will probably not be very many decades before the fashion in worship will change again and make the new church seem as unsuitable as its predecessor. There is little reason to suppose that liturgical change, which has been in progress since the days of the Apostles, is now about to "stop short," like art, in the words of J. S. Gilbert, at "the cultivated court of the Empress Josephine."

That being so, building committees and architects would be well advised to design durable churches with an eye to ongoing liturgical change. And since change often involves the recovery and revival of practices in times past, they would be well advised not to remove or destroy fine examples of altars, reredoses, and chancel screens when retrofitting old churches. There are better ways of adapting old churches to current liturgical practice than by making a clean sweep of the interiors and removing works of art or distinguished architectural features when with a little ingenuity they may be incorporated into a new scheme. A handsome chancel screen, for example, can be utilized as an effective reredos for a nave altar, and the former chancel can be converted into a weekday chapel, thus preserving and using the old high altar. St. James' in Great Barrington, Massachusetts, has one of the most beautiful American examples of the so-called English altar, a Gothic altar of stone with a magnificent carved and richly polychromed wooden reredos and riddel posts surmounted by gilded angels holding candlesticks. To destroy it by pulling the altar forward would be an act of vandalism. An outstanding period piece like this may well be greatly appreciated by generations yet unborn. Current liturgical requirements can be met simply by adding a freestanding altar in the chancel or at the head of the nave.

The Liturgical Background of the 1979 Prayer Book

The present *Book of Common Prayer* represents a confluence of two great liturgical currents: (1) the received liturgical tradition of Catholic Christendom as it has been practiced in Anglican use and especially as reflected in the 1549 Prayer Book and its successors; and (2) the insights, new and old, of the Liturgical Movement, which with the renewal of interest in biblical studies and with the Ecumenical Movement, constitute what the late Archbishop William Temple called the three great realities of the twentieth-century Church. Much of what remains constant as one Prayer Book replaces its predecessor, the vital continuity without which a liturgy remains merely academic, is attributable to the first, and much that is new as far as the 1928 Prayer Book is concerned is attributable to the second. In fairness, however, one must acknowledge that a certain amount of what appears new in the 1979 Prayer Book is, in fact, a recovery of parts of our Prayer Book tradition that have hitherto been ignored or discarded, sometimes inadvertently.*

---

*See Marion J. Hatchett, "Old Anglican Texts and Customs Revived in the Proposed Book of Common Prayer," *The Anglican* (Spring 1977).

"Change," as Richard Hooker wisely observed four centuries ago, "is not made without inconvenience, even from worse to better." Change, however, is easier to bear by those who are well informed and can distinguish between what is really an unbroken tradition since apostolic days and what is merely ephemeral. An example of the pain caused by failure to do so comes from the experience of the late James Pike. Shortly after his enthronement as bishop of California, Pike's attention was engrossed by the people of a particular parish who were up in arms. Indeed, they alleged that their new rector was destroying the tradition of the Episcopal church. Upon investigation, Bishop Pike found that the new incumbent had abruptly discontinued the practice of his revered predecessor of having the American flag carried in procession every Sunday at the 11:00 A.M. service. Many of the irate parishioners who had grown up under the old rector were astonished to learn that this innocent—and rather nice—custom was not an invariable ingredient of Episcopal worship. They had not learned the difference between the essentials of the Prayer Book tradition and ceremonial accretions that, however agreeable, are not generally necessary to salvation.

Many Things Change—A Few Do Not

Some things, to be sure, never change. God does not change: God is the same yesterday, today, and forever. Human nature, too, does not change—at least in its unredeemed state—as far back as historians and anthropologists can push our knowledge of the past. And to these may be added the essentials of Christian dogma, aptly defined as permanently necessary assertions about the faith. Essential as these are, they are few in number compared with the lesser doctrines that have been formulated at various times and periodically disputed by Christian leaders since the days of St. Peter and St. Paul. Dogma remains from age to age, but many teachings of the Church have been modified, revised, dropped, or revived as century succeeds century.

Although the essentials of baptism and the eucharist are constant and will remain until the end of the age, many of the details of worship are ephemeral and by proper authority can be changed, discarded, and restored as they are perceived to be edifying, or thought to be discordant, without in the least undermining the faith and worship of the catholic Church.

It can be asserted without fear of contradiction that periodic liturgical revision stands as a principle in Anglican worship, for the preface of the first English Prayer Book (1549) opened with this assertion: "There was never anything by the wit of man so well devised, or so sure established, which in continuance of time hath not been corrupted: as, among others, it may plainly appear by the common prayer [i.e. public worship] in the Church." Liturgical excellence can be maintained only by periodic revision, much as a white post exposed to the elements will remain white only if it is from time to time repainted. Also article 34 of the Thirty-nine Articles declared that "it is not necessary that Traditions and Ceremonies be in all places one, or utterly alike: for at all times they have been divers, and may be changed according to the diversity of countries, times, and men's manners, so that nothing be ordained against God's Word." And "every particular or national Church hath authority to ordain, change, and abolish Ceremonies or Rites of the Church ordained only by Man's authority, so that all things be done to edifying."

A New Imperative: Barrier-free Churches

"New occasions teach new duties," so the hymn by James Russell Lowell goes, and quite apart from liturgical change a new duty has been laid upon churches and those who are responsible for them, namely, to make them accessible to handicapped worshipers. We have always had "the halt, the lame, and the blind" with us, but in time past they were expected to stay home, where the priest could bring them the blessed sacrament periodically.

Little account, therefore, was taken of their needs when it came to designing churches and other public buildings. The English novelist, Anthony Trollope, on a visit to Washington in 1859, said some nice things about the capitol, but, speaking of the impressive flights of stairs on its east facade, he was candid enough to say that they were "more pleasing to the eye than to the feet." And many churches built in the second half of the nineteenth century were also adorned with imposing, but inconvenient, flights of steps. Inside, too, some of Gothic Revival style rejoiced in an elevated chancel that, whatever its merits in showing honor to the Holy Eucharist, made it hard for handicapped worshipers to make their way to the altar rail. But the day of ignoring the needs of the handicapped is over. With modern motorized wheelchairs and other marvels of prosthesis, they are commonly up and about and as anxious as their hale and sighted fellows to go to church.

The federal government and the state have long since recognized this turn of events and have decreed that public funds shall not be made available for any building that is not barrier-free to the handicapped. As a result, government offices, post offices, museums, and state and city universities now have ramps, elevators, and other facilities for those on crutches or in wheelchairs. It is a pity that the state rather than the Church took the initiative in this humane reform. The Church, however, is now following the good example set by the government. Along with other Christian bodies the Episcopal church has awakened to its "new duty," and the Episcopal Church Building Fund (ECBF), with money generously provided by the United Thank Offering, offers loans to Episcopal parishes for rendering existing buildings barrier-free.

A Short History of Liturgical Change

The great Anglican liturgical scholar, Dom Gregory Dix, O.S.B., in a famous statement declared:*

> At the heart of it all is the eucharistic action, a thing of absolute simplicity—the taking, blessing, breaking and giving of bread and the taking, blessing, and giving of a cup of wine and water, as these were first done with their new meaning by a young Jew before and after supper with His friends on the night before He died. Soon it was simplified still further, by leaving out the supper and combining the double grouping before and after it into a single rite. So the four-action Shape of the Liturgy was found by the end of the first century. He had told His friends to do this henceforward with the new meaning "for the *anamnesis*" of Him, and they have done it always since.
>
> Was ever another command so obeyed? For century after century, spreading slowly to every continent and country and among every race on earth, this action has been done, in every conceivable human circumstance, for every conceivable human need from infancy and before it to extreme old age and after it, from the pinnacles of earthly greatness to the refuge of fugitives in the caves and dens of the earth. Men have found no better thing than this to do for kings at their crowning and for criminals going to the scaffold; for armies in triumph or for a bride and bridegroom in a little country church; for the proclamation of a dogma or for a crop of good wheat; for the wisdom of the Parliament of a mighty nation or for a sick old woman afraid to die; for a schoolboy sitting an examination or for Columbus setting out to discover America. . . .

---

*Dom Gregory Dix, O.S.B., *The Shape of the Liturgy* (London: Dacre Press, 1945), 743–44.

And best of all, week by week and month by month, on a hundred thousand successive Sundays, faithfully, unfailingly, across all the parishes of Christendom, the pastors have done this just to make . . . the holy common people of God.

But what began as a thing of absolute simplicity eventually was enshrined in an ornate ceremonial setting—like a simple, unleavened Host in a jewelled monstrance. This was done, not to change the character of the sacrament, but to acknowledge its supreme importance in Christian worship. After all, if emperors, kings, and their ministers of state were habited in gorgeous robes and dined with gold and silver cups and plates, it scarcely seemed fitting to have the bishops, who were successors of the Apostles, and other clergy—all of them ministers of almighty God—attired any less magnificently or to prepare the altar for the foretaste of the heavenly banquet with common utensils of wood or pottery! And so the pendulum began to swing after Constantine gave recognition to Christianity.

The Pendulum Swings—From Constantine to the Middle Ages

From the fourth century onwards, Christians began to worship in large and impressive churches rather than in out-of-the-way nooks and in private homes. When the church became official it naturally sought to erect buildings that resembled the civic and imperial forms of the day. The building that was selected as a model for Christian churches was the basilica, which had been developed to house Roman courts of justice. (See Appendix A, Figure 1.) It was well adapted to worship because it provided a large meeting room separated from aisles or wings by pillars, and a semicircular apse that provided seating for the bishop and his attendant priests and deacons. The altar was located on the chord of the apse, or even in the body of the church, and hence was surrounded by worshipers, the clergy behind the altar and the laity in front of it, giving visual confirmation of the corporate nature of the eucharist.

In time, however, the empire fell—in the West at least—and the Dark Ages were gradually succeeded by the Middle Ages. By this time the Church was flourishing and influential. Its accumulating riches drew many into its service, and the numbers in holy orders grew enormously. In order to accommodate the burgeoning clergy, the apsidal ends of Romanesque churches were deepened, and by the time Gothic architecture came into its own, the chancel had become a regular feature of medieval churches. (See Appendix A, Figure 2.) The structural divider that visually separated the chancel from the nave had developed into the rood screen (which was comparable to the iconostasis in Eastern churches).

It was in the early centuries that another liturgical innovation began to affect the architectural setting of the eucharist. The rise of the cult of the saints, which was partly the result of looking back with reverent awe to the brave Christians who suffered torture and martydom during the years of persecution rather than forswear the Lord by offering incense to statues of pagan emperors, led to the adding of chapels to churches, for each holy relic was deemed worthy of its own altar. This, together with the custom of votive masses and the belief that each priest must celebrate the eucharist every day, led to the multiplication of altars.

As most people were illiterate in the Middle Ages, the clergy developed visuals such as statues and stained-glass windows as teaching devices. Shakespeare, in *As You Like It*, speaks of "tongues in trees, books in running brooks, sermons in stone" (11.i.12). They also attached symbolic importance to the architectural setting of the eucharist. Gothic churches often cruciform, were understood to represent the cross. Each church had five doors, representing the wounds of Christ, and they were often painted blood red. The nave, which held the people, stood for "the Church militant," the Church in the world. Fonts were placed near the west door to point up the fact that entry into the Church was by baptism. Pulpits and lecterns were located in the nave because Scripture was read and sermons preached in this world—not the next. The rood screen, with its great crucifix, separated chancel from nave and symbolized the fact that our Lord's Passion gave the faithful admittance to paradise. The chancel represented paradise, and the white-robed choristers placed there represented the choir of angels. The sanctuary, with its altar, stood for heaven itself and the heavenly banquet where the redeemed meet and enjoy the company of the risen and ascended Christ. In this scheme, a crucifix with the dead body of our Lord would be appropriate only in the nave, near the pulpit, or on the rood screen. If he is depicted above or behind the altar, it should of course be as the risen, not the dead, Christ, for it is Christ in majesty with whom we have to do the eucharist. But in the course of the Middle Ages, the increasing emphasis on our Lord's atoning sacrifice as the means of our salvation, and the medieval preoccupation with sin and death, resulted in a partial breakdown of this scheme and the appearance of crucifixes with the corpus in the sanctuary. This also seemed appropriate as the concept of the eucharist as a sacrifice, rather than a heavenly banquet, became dominant.

By the late Middle Ages the corporate nature of the eucharist had been lost sight of, and the architectural setting of worship had developed along other lines. Over the centuries congregational participation had declined, partly because the liturgy continued to be in Latin long after the rise of modern languages and partly because the musical setting of worship had gradually been elaborated and could no longer be sung by the people. In consequence, the ceremonial of the eucharist suggested that the celebrant was speaking to God on behalf of the people and performing the eucharistic action *for* them rather than *with* them. Small wonder, then, that instead of facing the people from behind the altar while celebrating, the celebrant had shifted his position to the front of the altar with his back to the people! Interestingly enough, this change resulted in chasubles being more richly decorated on the back than on the front. As nothing would be gained by reciting the rite in a loud voice, for Latin was understood only by ecclesiastics, lawyers, and physicians, priests fell into the habit of speaking in a low voice. And the chancel was peopled with a variety of clerics and religious in minor as well as major orders and with trained choristers who alone could cope with the elaborate polyphonic musical settings of the liturgy that had been developed over the centuries as an offering to the glory of God.

The worshipers in the nave usually could neither hear the eucharistic prayer, nor participate in the music as their ancestors had done when simple plainsong was used. They were therefore obliged to content themselves with private prayer and devotions such as the rosary until the sound of the sacring bell galvanized their attention by signifying the high point of the partially invisible and inaudible celebration. It is hardly surprising that the idea spread abroad that the eucharist, instead of being a corporate action of the whole body of the faithful, was something done by the clergy for the benefit of the laity.

The Pendulum Swings Back—From 1549 to Sir Christopher Wren

The sixteenth century reformers tried to correct this situation and to recover early Christian practice. Because of the innate conservatism of the people, however, they were only partially successful. A notable instance of their failure was their inability to persuade people to receive Holy Communion frequently, instead of only once a year, as had been the normal medieval practice. We do not ordinarily think of Calvinists as being in favor of a weekly eucharist. But John Calvin, in his *Institutes*, declared that "it was not ordained to be received only once a year . . . rather, it was ordained to be frequently used among all Christians in order that they might frequently return in memory to Christ's Passion . . . [and] by it to nourish mutual love, and . . . give witness to this love." And he believed that whenever and wherever Christians gathered together, the word should be read and preached and Holy Communion administered.

The English reformers also tried to discourage noncommunicating attendance at the eucharist by insisting that the priest celebrate it only when there were at least a few people who intended to receive. They were to notify the priest the day before so that he could provide sufficient bread and wine to consecrate and so that, having committed themselves ahead of time, they might have time and a motive to prepare themselves spiritually to receive the Blessed Sacrament. These worthwhile objectives, however, foundered upon the reef of conservatism. Ultimately, the Church of England was obliged to lower its sights and settle for the requirement that every communicant receive the sacrament at least three times each year, including Easter.

In other respects, Thomas Cranmer, Archbishop of Canterbury 1532-1553, was more successful in recovering a sense of corporateness in worship. His 1549 *Book of Common Prayer* anticipated some of the objectives of the later Liturgical Movement. By simplifying the services and translating them into English, he made it possible for the worshipers in the nave to understand the language of the liturgy. He also provided congregational responses, instead of allowing the professionals in the chancel to make the responses for the congregation. And in 1550 he got John Merbecke, the organist of St. George's Chapel, Windsor, to compose and publish *The Book of Common Prayer Noted* in which simple plainsong was adapted to the 1549 liturgy on the principle of one note to a syllable, thus enabling the people for the first time in centuries to join in the singing of those parts of the service that were formerly monopolized by trained choirs.

Once the liturgy was again in the tongue of the people, the hearing of the rite took on a new importance, and that in turn created a need for a different architectural setting for worship. In the Middle Ages, when the liturgy was in Latin, it was enough if the people in the nave could, in Sir Christopher Wren's words, "hear the Murmer of the Mass," but with the appearance of the English Mass in 1549, they now wished and expected to hear the words spoken by the priest. This was achieved, or at least facilitated, by persuading the clergy to speak distinctly and in a loud voice, by clearing away the medieval chantry chapels now now longer needed, and by moving much of the liturgical action from the far end of the chancel to the front of it or to the nave.

The medieval stone altars, which were associated with the now rejected concept of the "sacrifice of the Mass," were replaced by wooden holy tables that were portable and could be moved nearer the people. Matins, the litany, and a large part of the eucharist (i.e., down to the offertory) were transferred to the nave in the interests of audibility. At the time of the offertory, the priest, accompanied by the intending communicants, went to the chancel and stood or knelt around the holy table, so that all could see and hear the consecration. Out of service time, the altar was returned to its customary place at the east end. In this way, the interiors of England's medieval churches were retrofitted in order to adapt them to the *Book of Common Prayer.*

The Renaissance brought with it a revival of classical culture, which, among other things, awakened interest in the architecture of the ancient Greeks and Romans, including pagan temples that predated the late Roman basilica that had provided a model for early Christian churches. Renaissance architects revived the temple form and adapted it to Christian worship in the sixteenth and seventeenth centuries. Among the most notable examples of neoclassical churches are St. Peter's in Rome and St. Paul's in London. But Anglican and Roman liturgical practices diverged after the Reformation. The Roman rite retained its Latin and developed its ceremonial along lines of visual imagery, whereas the Anglican liturgy was translated into English, and its ceremonial emphasis was auditory rather than visual.

Sweeping away rood screens inherited from the Middle Ages, the Roman authorities created the "dramatic altar" set against an ornate reredos that visually dominated the interior. It was a radical departure from the "mysterious altar" of the medieval church, which was remote and shrouded from view by the rood screen, a deep chancel, riddel curtains, clouds of incense, and the "dim, religious light" of flickering candles and stained-glass windows. The ultimate outgrowth of Renaissance classicism was the baroque style, which on the continent was an exuberant proclamation of the Counter-Reformation. It has been said that it had for its prototype not the pagan temple but the theatre, which, thanks to the emergence of grand opera, became the cultural focus of the eighteenth century.

In England, on the other hand, where great emphasis was placed on hearing, the ecclesiastical authorities chose to retain the medieval rood screens. They did so, apparently, because they accepted the inherited concept, which the Counter-Reformation church rejected, that a church consisted of two quite distinct rooms that the chancel screen visually divided, one from the other. The nave was the place for the ministry of the word, and the chancel the place for the celebration of the eucharist and the reception of the Blessed Sacrament.

The practice of moving the portable holy table to the chancel for the sacrament and returning it to the east wall after the service eventually encountered opposition from conservative church members on the ostensible grounds that it resulted in a decline in reverence for the altar as a sacred object. Puritans, of course, disliked the idea of blessing material things, and they were said to have no compunction about using the holy table to cast up churchwarden accounts or as a desk for the master of the parochial school on weekdays. As it usually took less to bring Archbishop Laud to a boil, that redoubtable prelate took steps to put an end to the aberration by ordering altars left permanently in their traditional location and by requiring them to be railed in to protect them from profanation by dogs and Puritans!

The Caroline divines generally favored a revival of medieval ceremonial and, among other things, elicited attacks by the Puritans for using incense, medieval-style chalices, and vestments that had not been in common use for nearly a century. Contrary to the general direction in which things were moving in the early seventeenth century, the reaction of the Caroline divines in the reign of Charles I, with his approval, created a minirevival of medieval ceremonial, and Archbishop Laud was the presiding genius of this Catholic upsurge. But the timing was bad. It came just as the Puritans were growing in number and power. The archbishop and his king, although dedicated church members and saintly in their personal character, were far from politically adept. They were beheaded and their revival eclipsed during Cromwell's ascendancy, but, of course, the Laudian revival arose like a phoenix from its ashes after the Restoration of Charles II in 1660.

The Great Fire of London in 1666 had an unforeseen repercussion in the realm of ecclesiastical architecture. Until then, the large number of surviving medieval churches—more than 9,000—was generally sufficient for the needs of the established church, once these had been retrofitted. But the Great Fire destroyed no fewer than eighty-six London churches, including old St. Paul's Cathedral. This created, for the first time since the Reformation, a need to build a large number of churches in England. Sir Christopher Wren, England's greatest architect, was assigned the task of designing and building their replacements, and he used the opportunity to create new forms intended to meet the liturgical requirements of the *Book of Common Prayer* more effectively than retrofitted medieval churches.

He chose the classical style—basically the temple form that was already in use on the continent—but for quite different reasons. The objective of Bramante's St. Peter's in Rome, for example, was more visual than auditory. What was desired was a grand setting for an impressive altar and for magnificent ceremonial. Wren's objective, on the other hand, was to find the ideal form for an auditory church in which all the worshipers could hear the words of the liturgy and be able to participate in the congregational responses. So successful was Wren in adapting classical forms to Prayer Book worship that his churches were widely copied, both in England and in America. His style dominated Anglican ecclesiastical architecture for a century and a half, until it was overwhelmed by the rising tide of the Gothic Revival in the middle of the nineteenth century.

The Pendulum Hangs Still—The Received Tradition in America

English people who left their native shores and settled in the American colonies were usually nostalgic about England's green and pleasant land. Hence it was natural for them to build churches in the New World that resembled, as far as possible, those they had left behind. As a result, most colonial churches were recognizable as simplified variants of the current style in the mother country. For the first century and a half or more, Americans were not able to build anything as large or as fine as the best churches in London —at least, not until the erection of King's Chapel, Boston (1749-54), St. Michael's, Charleston (1752-61), and Christ Church, Philadelphia (1727-44). But they did provide their simple country churches with much the same interior arrangement for worship. (See Appendix A, Figure 3.)

Colonial churches, although sometimes cruciform (like Bruton Parish Church in Williamsburg), were usually rectangular with a central aisle and with the altar at the east end—often in a shallow chancel—and provided with altar rails. A massive pulpit, usually with one or two reading desks attached (for the priest and the clerk), was located on a side wall of the nave or, occasionally, in the central aisle of the nave in front of the altar (as in Trinity at Newport, Rhode Island). The latter was especially practical in churches with side galleries. Parish choirs, wearing street attire, not surplices, sat in a rear gallery where the organ, if the church was fortunate enough to have one, was customarily located. This arrangement provided a practical setting for hearing as well as seeing the liturgical action. When pulpits were in the aisle in front of the altar, there was no thought of exalting the Word over the sacrament or of showing disrespect to the altar. It was done solely for practical reasons because this location made it easier for all the worshipers, including those in the gallery, to see and hear the liturgy and the sermon. In addition, in a small church this placement of the three-decker prevented it from obscuring a view of the altar, which would have been the case if it were against a wall of the nave.

Galleries were common in colonial churches because these churches were usually built to meet current needs, whereas the population was growing by leaps and bounds. No sooner was a church built than it proved to be too small. In consequence, seating capacity was periodically increased by adding galleries and building wings. A good example is St. Anne's, Annapolis, built in 1699–1704, when Maryland's "metropolis" was a town of only 250 inhabitants. As the town grew, the original brick church, which was sixty-five feet by thirty feet, soon needed more seating capacity. In 1723 a group of parishioners obtained permission to build a gallery at their own expense, and five years later another was authorized by the vestry. By 1734 a transept had been added, and in 1740 the church was enlarged and eleven more pews added to the gallery. In 1761 yet another gallery was built for the newly acquired organ, the organist, and the choir. It was said that all these galleries enabled the church to hold "almost as many above as below."

A word needs to be said about the massive three-deckers that visually dominated the interiors of eighteenth-century churches. For Anglicans of that day, the pulpit had a somewhat different connotation than it does for us. Since Victorian days, it has been associated exclusively with preaching, but for our Caroline and

15

Georgian forebears it stood as much for the prayer book liturgy as for sermons, because, as we have seen, it was the practice of the church before the Ecclesiologists and Ritualists to read most of the service—matins, litany, and ante-communion—from the three-decker. The priest left the massive structure to go to the altar at the offertory, and those who intended to receive the sacrament—usually only a small part of the congregation—accompanied him to the altar rail. Perhaps the curious phrase "filling the pulpit" to describe the function of a supply priest—which makes modern day Episcopalians cringe—is a vestige of pre-Victorian times when the pulpit was a symbol of the church's "incomparable" liturgy no less than of preaching!

Because of the premium on space in crowded colonial churches and because of the effective transfer of most of the Prayer Book liturgy to the three-decker pulpit, the chancel in American churches became smaller as the years passed. By the late colonial period it had been reduced to a shallow apse or omitted altogether. Indeed, by the end of the eighteenth century the altar was commonly located at the east end of a rectangular church and separated from the nave only by its rails. Wren's desire to create a church "fitted for Auditories" had carried the day.

The Pendulum Vibrates Wildly—Evanglicals and Ecclesiologists

With the rise of the Evangelical Movement in the late eighteenth century and its period of maximum influence in the first third of the nineteenth century, a new force was unleashed that had a profound effect upon Anglican worship. Indeed, the interior arrangement of churches built or retrofitted by the Evangelicals represents a high watermark of departure from the medieval setting for worship. (See Appendix A, Figure 4.) The Evangelicals laid unprecedented stress upon preaching and were less influenced by tradition and by a sense of obligation to conform to the rubrics of the Prayer Book than either their predecessors or their successors. In consequence, they often rearranged church interiors and built new ones in accordance with what they considered important. Although chiefly the product of the Evangelicals, this setting of worship was not entirely a matter of churchmanship. It was also promoted by such High Churchmen as bishops Hobart and Dehon, who liked the idea of keeping the altar and font, as well as the pulpit, constantly before the people.

The Evangelicals abandoned the concept of the separation

between the chancel and the nave and scrapped the idea of having three distinct liturgical centers. Instead, they consolidated pulpit, altar, and font in one center, placing a small table in front of and below the pulpit, which visually dominated the interior. Instead of a stone font, required by Anglican canon law, they often used a silver bowl, placed on the communion table, for baptisms. Lacking enthusiasm for processions for which the Prayer Book made provision, they often eliminated the central aisle and filled the body of the church with a block of pews, thus rendering their churches hardly distinguishable from those of Congregationalists, Methodists, and Baptists. The auditory principle reached its apogee in their churches, and their setting of worship proclaimed their conviction that it was less a matter of participation in an action than it was of speaking and hearing. Anglican worship had never been so nearly stripped of ceremonial or religion so completely intellectualized as it was by the Evangelicals a century and a half ago. But by eliminating chancels and bringing altar and people close together, the Evangelicals anticipated one of the objectives of the twentieth-century Liturgical Movement.

But liturgy is not static. It is in a state of continual change. Even when the ritual (i.e., the words) is more or less fixed, as in the *Book of Common Prayer*, the attitudes of the worshipers tend to bring about changes in the ceremonial that accompany and interpret the rite. With any considerable change in ceremonial, the need arises to rearrange church interiors to accommodate it. No sooner had the Evangelicals reached the apex of their influence than the movement that bears their name lost steam and began to decline. When that happened, it was soon overtaken by another movement that began in England in the 1830s and became dominant by the end of the century. Indeed, by 1900 almost every Anglican church from the Orkneys to Land's End and from Alaska to New Zealand had undergone retrofitting in response to the Catholic Revival.

The groundswell began modestly enough with a sermon preached at Oxford in 1833 by a mild-mannered professor of poetry, John Keble. In this sermon, entitled "National Apostasy," Keble deplored the current state of the Church of England and the decline of the nation from Catholic faith and practice. He was speaking, of course, of the Catholic aspect of Anglicanism that had been enunciated by Archbishop Laud and the Caroline divines and not of the ethos of the contemporary continental church of Rome. This attracted an inordinate amount of attention and inaugurated the Oxford Movement, which found its expression in the publication of ninety *Tracts For The Times* from 1833 to 1841, thereby earning the name "Tractarians" for participants in the movement. They stressed the historical continuity of the English church with Catholic Christianity of the apostolic and patristic periods and upheld a high concept of the authority of the Church, of the claims of the episcopate, and of the nature of the sacraments. The Tractarians, however, were concerned chiefly with doctrine rather than with liturgy. It remained for their successors, the Ritualists, in a later phase of the Oxford Movement to revive elaborate medieval ceremonial, including eucharistic vestments, candles, incense, and the like, as fitting expressions of the doctrinal position of the Tractarians.

Meanwhile, another movement began at Cambridge that was destined to give architectural expression to the Catholic revival. It was founded in 1839 by John Mason Neale and Benjamin Webb, undergraduates at the university, under the name Cambridge Camden Society. Its avowed purpose was studying ecclesiastical art. In a very short time it was joined by a number of prominent church members, and by 1841 it began to issue a monthly periodical, *The Ecclesiologist*. The name was derived from "ecclesiology," which was defined as the science of the building and decoration of churches. In 1846 its headquarters were moved to London and its name changed to the Ecclesiological Society. The movement represented a reaction and revival. Reacting against lethargy, irreverence, and the ugliness of the Industrial Revolution and aided by the Romantic Movement in literature and the popular novels of Sir Walter Scott, the Ecclesiologists undertook to revive the medieval glory of the English church.

They also revolted against the classical revival styles that had been used for churches since Wren's day and urged the abandonment of auditory buildings. Instead, they chose the Gothic, two-roomed church with its deep chancel, the "decorated" style that flourished between 1260 and 1360, and they insisted that this, and only this, was the "correct" model for Anglican churches. (See Appendix A, Figure 5.)

Their impact on the Church was phenomenal and greatly stimulated interest in ecclesiastical architecture and traditional medieval worship. For that reason, the Ecclesiologists worked hand in glove with the Ritualists in bringing about a ceremonial revival in the Church of England in the second half of the nineteenth century.

James F. White, in his admirable study *The Cambridge Movement,* describes the remarkable transformation that had taken place by the end of Queen Victoria's reign: "The appearance of England's churches had been radically altered and a revolution had occured in the way in which worship was conducted in them. Indeed, so widespread were the changes in this period, that it is now difficult to visualize the arrangement of the average Anglican parish church of the 1830s or the manner in which the services were held." And this was accomplished without a revision of the Prayer Book!

Spokespersons for the Church of England in the reign of Queen Elizabeth I and the Stuarts had rejoiced in the name of "Catholic," which they identified with the undivided Church of apostolic and patristic times, and they accepted as binding the decisions of the first six ecumenical councils, i.e., through that of Constantinople in A.D. 680–81. (On that account, every England sovereign at his or her coronation receives a ring described as "the seal of Catholic Faith.") But they also rejoiced in the name "Protestant," which they identified with a wholesome elimination of corrupt accretions in the Western church since A.D. 681. The amiable and devout physician Sir Thomas Browne (1605–82) likened this to a ship having barnacles scraped from its hull. And so every sovereign also promises to maintain "the Protestant Reformed Religion established by law." The latter, clearly, was regarded as synonymous with the Catholic faith. These spokespersons, and the rank and file of the Church of England, also harbored a deep distrust of the Counter-Reformation church because of its power and ever-present threat to the English church and state and because it appeared to glory in the corrupt accretions that Anglicans had sloughed off.

Savants of the Age of Reason, both church members and agnostics, deplored the Middle Ages as a time of rampant superstition, and they identified Gothic architecture and the unreformed Church of Rome with it. But the Romantic Movement and the Ecclesiologists wrought a dramatic reversal of that perception. Before the end of the nineteenth century, English-speaking people generally and Anglicans in particular had become enchanted by medieval ways and sought to emulate their romanticised view of them. Gothic architecture was now perceived to be the only proper style for churches and medieval designs the only proper model for chasubles, copes, and chalices.

As the "Romish" church was still under the spell of the baroque style, Anglicans began to see themselves as the legitimate heirs of the medieval church, whereas Roman Catholics, despite their unbroken descent from patristic times, had slipped their medieval cables by casting off Gothic design in favor of baroque, by exalting papal authority above that of general councils, and by adding novelties to ancient Catholic dogma. Contrary to all expectation, the Middle Ages, which for three centuries had been regarded as the epitome of ecclesiastical corruption and superstition, suddenly (or at least in a short period of time) came to be seen as the great Age of Faith and the acme of church architecture!

With this identification of the Church of England with medieval ways and the assertion of its unbroken descent from the church of St. Augustine and the *Ecclesia Anglicana* of Magna Carta, Anglicans became increasingly uncomfortable with the appellation "Protestant," which by the nineteenth century had come to be associated primarily, if not exclusively, with the churches of the Reformation. In consequence, Anglicans have been inclined to dissociate their church from the name "Protestant," not, of course, in its seventeenth-century sense, but certainly from the more recent shades of meaning that have been assigned to the word in popular parlance.

The Pendulum Swings Again—Percy Dearmer and the Society of SS. Peter and Paul

The Catholic Revival generated in the Church of England by the Ritualists and Ecclesiologists, although remarkably successful, resulted in confusion. There was a lack of accurate knowledge about medieval liturgy and architecture, and this led many church architects to indulge in flights of fancy or else to look to contemporary continental sources for inspiration, with the result that by the 1890s details of design and practice were, in Peter Anson's words, "fussy and restless."

In general, parish priests wished to obey the rubric that authorized the retention of those ornaments and vestments that were in use "in the second year of the reign of Edward VI," i.e., between January 28, 1548, and January 27, 1549. But no one seemed to have a clear idea what they were. Hence, there was a great need for scholarly work and publication in this field. To meet the need, J. T. Micklethwaite brought out his influential book, *The Ornaments of the Rubric* in 1897. It was the first of a series of studies that are still being added to each year known as *Alcuin Club Tracts*, devoted to an objective and practical study of "ceremonial and the arrangement of churches, their furniture and ornaments, in accordance with the rubrics of the *Book of Common Prayer*."

Micklethwaite came up with a long and astonishing list of ornaments that were authorized by the rubric, including riddel curtains for the altar, a hanging pyx for the Reserved Sacrament, two candles on the altar and one on each side of it, as well as additional candles at great festivals. He also adduced documentary evidence for monstrances, houseling cloths, lenten veils, and other items that had been in disuse for more than three centuries. And in his final words he sounded the keynote of what would be an article of faith for the Alcuin Club and its chief popularizer, Percy Dearmer: "The substitution of foreign (i.e., Roman Catholic) ornaments is mischievous from the countenance it gives to those who profess to see in the present revival within the Church of England only an imitation of the Church of Rome. And we do not want their things, our own are better."

The Alcuin Club publications were influential but reached only a limited circle of ecclesiastical scholars. What was needed was someone to popularize the club's discoveries, and that person was Percy Dearmer (1867–1936), a scholarly priest who later became a professor of ecclesiastical art at King's College, London, and a canon of Westminster. Revolting against the eclectic Anglo-Catholic ceremonial in the church where he had been a curate, he readily espoused Micklethwaite's dictum and set about to disseminate the findings of the Alcuin Club antiquarians. In 1899 he published his *Parson's Handbook,* the object of which, as he stated it in the introduction, was "to help, in however humble a way, towards remedying the lamentable confusion, lawlessness and vulgarity which are conspicuous at this time." In particular, he appealed to the church authorities to take advantage of the talents of the best artists and craftsmen in the land rather than be "content with decoration that is the ridicule of competent artists, or is ignored by them as not being even amusing." The *Parson's Handbook* sold in large numbers and went through twelve editions before his death in 1936. Written in a charming and humorous vein, it proved to be both practical and successful.

More than any single writer, Dearmer popularized the "English altar" and ceremonial that was rooted in English liturgical and ecclesiological history, free from what he called the "anomalous, irreverent, tawdry, and grotesque." Within half a century his book and the example provided by his London parish, St. Mary the Virgin, Primrose Hill, enjoyed the honor of being followed in thousands of churches throughout the Anglican Communion. Among the many things that have been attributed to his influence, besides the English altar, are the widespread removal of gradines and the placing of only two candlesticks on the altar, the replacement of brass missal stands by cushions covered with damask, the recovery of apparels on albs and amices, and the restoration of the traditional choir habit of the clergy (i.e., cassock, surplice, hood, and tippet), which had come down unbroken from the Middle Ages to the early Victorian period and had only then been largely abandoned.

His followers, sometimes known as "Dearmerites," perpetuated his views and objectives by founding the Anglican Society in England in 1926 and its American counterpart in 1932. The periodical of the former is *The Anglican Catholic* and of the latter, *The Anglican.*

Despite the phenomenal success of Dearmer and the Alcuin Club tracts, not all Anglo-Catholics were willing to dance to their tune. Some resisted the medievalism of the Ecclesiologists, reflected in the agenda of the Dearmerites, and chose to stand by the baroque concepts that still dominated the continental Roman Catholic church. Those who opposed Dearmer's vision of "the holiness of beauty and the beauty of holiness" derided his views as "British Museum religion" and in 1911 organized the Society of SS. Peter and Paul to launch a crusade against the principles of the Alcuin Club. Needless to say, their objective was not to return to medieval practice but to advance in the direction of what the Anglican church might have been had there been no Reformation. In short, they favored copying the current styles and practices of the Roman church on the continent. Not being able to agree on anything so hypothetical, they settled on baroque decor as the only "correct" way of designing Anglican churches and maintained that this was better than Dearmer's medieval revival. In effect, they held the seventeenth and eighteenth centuries to be superior to the fifteenth and sixteenth centuries, and they favored fiddleback chasubles and short cottas adorned with lace, in protest against the long, full, flowing vestments heralded by the Alcuin Club and the advocates of the *Parons' Handbook.* Peter Anson waggishly points out that they had the advantage of appearing to be in greater rapport with the times because albs in approved Society of SS. Peter and Paul churches "resembled Victorian lace curtains!"

For want of an effective popularizer like Percy Dearmer, the Society of SS. Peter and Paul failed to attract the attention of large numbers of Anglican priests and hence did not enjoy the phenomenal success of its adversaries. But it did exert influence among the extreme Anglo-Catholic wing of the church by giving such church members what they wanted and by articulating opposition to their opponents.

The Pendulum Swings Back Again—The Liturgical Movement

The most notable changes brought about in the twentieth century have been the result of the Liturgical Movement, the object of which is the recovery of the concept of the eucharist as a corporate action and the restoration of the active participation of the people in the worship of the Church. Its earliest stirrings began with Dom Prosper Louis Gueranger (1805-75), a French priest who was responsible for reestablishing the Benedictine order in France, became the first abbot of the monastery at Solesmes in 1837, and was keenly interested in liturgical matters. But the chief impetus came from the directions of Pope Pius X relating to church music (in 1903) and to his promotion of eucharistic piety and frequent communion. Among the aims of the movement is the education of the laity to a deeper appreciation of the liturgy, to a better understanding of the church year, and, as a result, to a closer connection between liturgical worship and private devotion. In the Anglican church, the Ritualists, who succeeded the Tractarians and sought to give liturgical expression to their doctrinal position, had succeeded in restoring the idea that the eucharist was central in the church's worship, but they had not succeeded in restoring the widespread participation of the people. That remained for the Liturgical Movement to accomplish.

In order to give visual expression to the corporate nature of the eucharist, this movement sought to go behind the neomedievalism of the Ritualists and Ecclesiologists to the practice of early Christian times when priests and people gathered around the altar and together celebrated the eucharist. (See Appendix A, Figure 6.) They favored the use of freestanding altars nearer the people than the east end of the church. And they revived the early Christian practice of celebrating from behind the altar facing the people. This change, of course, constituted the abandonment of the Anglican principle, enunciated at the Savoy Conference in 1661, that the priest should face east when speaking to God in prayer and west when speaking to the people in exhortation and invitation. Facing east in prayer implies that God is somewhere beyond the east end of the church, whereas facing the people from behind the altar, they maintain, implies that our Lord is in the midst of the gathered Church. And this is more appropriate to the doctrine of the real presence of Christ and of our Lord's promise to be in their *midst* whenever two or three are gathered in his name.

It was not long before new churches were erected without deep chancels filled with choir stalls, and old ones were retrofitted to achieve the same effect. Organs and choirs in ever-increasing numbers have been moved back to the west gallery, thus providing a spacious setting for a freestanding altar and for seating accommodations for the celebrant and his or her attending ministers of the altar, in full view of the worshipers in the nave.

This rearrangement of the architectural setting of the worship in older churches often restores their interiors in some ways to something like their original design before the passionate Ecclesiologists decreed deep chancels for the altar and for the organist and choristers. It also brings with it two important benefits: organs stashed behind chancel walls often suffer a substantial loss of volume or tone, whereas organs in rear galleries do not. In consequence, less expensive instruments acoustically well-located are more effective than larger and more costly ones impacted behind walls with only a small, screened aperture to serve as a conduit for the sound.

The other benefit accruing from the removal of choir and organ to the rear gallery, and the consequent freeing of the chancel of the clutter of choir stalls, is that space is made available around the altar to accommodate the array of functionaries such as curates, acolytes, crucifers, banner bearers, taperers, and thurifers, that were the product of the Victorian Ritualists, as well as the newer chalice bearers and, possibly, lectors.

As new wine bursts old skins, this proliferation of ministers of the altar put an unbearable strain on the small sanctuaries of old churches, and retrofitting became a widespread necessity in order to adapt them to the new ceremonial and provide space where it was needed. Churches that were retrofitted in the second half of the nineteenth century to meet the standards of the Ecclesiologists now had to be rearranged once more, for, as architects continually remind us, "form follows function," and when the function changes, so must the form.

The remainder of this book deals specifically with items related to the setting of worship under headings arranged in alphabetical order. In each case, where applicable, the conclusions of the liturgical scholar Marion J. Hatchett concerning the "Architectural Implications of the Book of Common Prayer 1979" are included in order to make the best advice available to the reader. His article by that title first appeared in the *Occasional Papers of the Standing Liturgical Commission of the Episcopal Church* (December 1984). It has since been reprinted in *The Anglican* (Winter 1984) and in *Open* (August 1985), the periodical of the Associated Parishes for Liturgy and Mission.

Individual Topics

ALTARS (see also SIDE ALTARS)

In the early centuries of the Church, altars were in the form of wooden tables echoing the "supper" aspect of the eucharist in apostolic days. But with the rise of the cult of martyrs in the fourth century this began to change. The practice of celebrating the eucharist at or near the tomb of a saint resulted in linking an altar with a tomb, thereby giving perference to stone altars. In some cases, altars were built over a martyr's grave. In others, the remains of a saint were interred beneath an altar. Some altars had a relic buried in the top of the altar. In time, custom required that no altar be used without such a relic or, if one could not be obtained, then with a consecrated host. These practices made stone altars—or at least stone mensas—almost universal. A few altars in medieval England are known to have been made of wood, but they were exceptional vestiges of pre-conquest days.

Early Christian altars varied in shape. Some were square, some round, and a few were semicircular. In time, however, they tended to become cube-shaped, i.e., of approximately equal dimensions, and they were usually dignified by a canopy called a "ciborium," which, with its supporting columns, was of wood, stone, or precious metal. In western Europe there was a tendency to lengthen the altars, particularly in larger churches, presumably so that they wouldn't be dwarfed by the size of the edifice, and possibly to accommodate wax candles that were substituted for oil lamps when the Church moved inland away from the Mediterranean basin where olive trees grew.

The altar in Tewkesbury Abbey, for example, was thirteen feet long, and that of the Lady Chapel at Ely no less than sixteen feet in length. In consequence of this development, the earlier ciborium was dismantled. The corner posts were retained and sometimes topped with carved angels holding candles, and the posts were connected by rods that supported riddel curtains. The canopy was raised, elongated, and suspended from the ceiling or by wall brackets. This late medieval Gothic altar later became the ideal of the Dearmerites and was called an "English altar," mistakenly, for it was prevalent throughout northern Europe by the end of the Middle Ages.

Originally there was only one altar in a church and one celebration of the eucharist in any church on any day, as is true to this day in Eastern Orthodox churches. But in the course of the Middle Ages, the Western church multiplied altars in churches, especially those associated with monastic orders or with guilds, as a result of the growth of chantry chapels where daily eucharists were offered by privately endowed priests for the repose of the soul of the benefactor. Indeed, the medieval emphasis on sin and death and the development of the doctrine of purgatory wrought a conspicuous change in the interior appearance of parish churches everywhere, cluttering them with ever-increasing numbers of chapels and altars.

Another medieval development eliminated the freestanding altars of early Christian churches. In the West, it came to be placed against a wall or a screen at the east end of the church, which was the result of the abandonment of the westward position of the celebrant. Now that he stood with his back to the people, there was no need to provide space for him behind the altar, and hence it could without inconvenience be placed against the east wall.

It is worth mentioning that the use of a cross and candlesticks on the altar was a medieval innovation arising out of the custom of carrying them in procession and placing them on the pavement around the altar during services. It was not until the end of the Middle Ages that these things were commonly placed on the altar itself and came to be regarded as ornaments. The idea that all altars should have a cross standing on them is deeply rooted in the minds of most modern Episcopalians, but, in fact, it was a fantasy of the Victorian Ecclesiologists. The same is true of the idea, espoused by many Anglo-Catholics, that there should always be six candlesticks on the altar. Far from being medieval, it grew out of the Counter-Reformation and remained a peculiarity of the Roman church until overzealous Ritualists of the Victorian age adopted it in the mistaken notion that it was medieval and, therefore, a proper part of the Anglican heritage.

Also, at the risk of demythologizing the ideas of many altar guild members, it is worth mentioning that flower vases were not used on altars until Victorian days. Before that time, flowers were strewn on the pavement before altars or hung in garlands on the walls, especially at Christmas and Easter. Altars were traditionally hung with rich frontals of costly materials, often decorated with gold fringe. Flowers, therefore, were scarcely needed to dignify altars or to add a note of color. The Evangelicals, however, were uninterested in designing elegant frontals. Hence, they often let the old ones wear out and neglected to replace them. The resulting use of bare altars ultimately led people to try to correct the offense by crowding colorful flowers on their altars.

The sixteenth century reformers, in their zeal to counteract the medieval doctrine of the sacrifice of the mass, and in the interest of making altars portable so they could be moved nearer the people, endeavored to eliminate stone altars from English churches. They replaced them with wooden tables that could be moved into the chancel where communicants could assemble and be close to the celebrant and able to hear the prayer of consecration and see the manual acts.

The 1549 Prayer Book, following medieval practice, directed the priest to stand at the middle of the altar to begin the eucharist, "commonly called the Mass." The next year, under pressure from the Reforming party, the council, acting in the name of the boy king, Edward VI, ordered all stone altars taken down and, instead, tables "set up in some convenient part of the church." Accordingly, the 1552 Prayer Book directed the priest to stand on the north side of the holy table to begin the eucharist, now called the Lord's Supper or Holy Communion. Queen Mary, who reigned from 1553 to 1558, ordered the old altars restored and placed in their traditional location at the east end. When Elizabeth I came to the throne, she declared in true *via media* style (which she helped to create) that "there seemeth no matter of great moment whether the altar be removed or not, saving for uniformity." Then she went on to lay down expressly that "the Holy Table be set in the place where the altar stood . . . saving when the Communion of the Sacrament is to be distributed, at which time the same shall be so placed in good sort [i.e., as may be convenient] within the Chancel," and then to "be placed where it stood before," i.e., against the east wall.

For the next half century, altars were made of wood in table form and were portable so that they could be moved to the chancel for the eucharist and placed in an east-west axis. This curious practice explains the rubric in all editions of the Prayer Book from 1552 to 1662 directing the celebrant to begin the eucharist standing on the north side of the holy table. The effect intended, of course, was that the priest occupied the same position relative to the altar as he had when it stood altar-wise on a north-south axis at the east end of the church.

In the days of Charles I when there was a High Church revival under Archbishop Laud and the Caroline divines, the custom of bringing the holy table into the chancel at the time of communion was discouraged and eventually prohibited. Thereafter, except for the ascendancy of the Puritans under Cromwell, altars remained at all times at the east end as in the days before 1550 and were occasionally made of stone. Laud also urged the construction of altar rails in every parish church, which would have been impracticable and unnecessary while portable altars were regularly shuttled between the east wall and the chancel. Oddly enough, the 1662 Prayer Book retained the rubric requiring the priest to begin the eucharist standing at the north side of the altar. It was probably inadvertent on the part of the revisers, who had more pressing matters to attend to. But Anglicans, being as they are, adopted the habit of standing at the north end of the altar to begin the eucharist. They have continued this habit down to comparatively recent times as a kind of shibboleth to separate strict observers of the rubric from the more cavalier approach of those, especially the Victorian Ritualists, who perceived the retention of the old rubric to be an error and therefore ignored it.

This quaint Elizabethan experiment of moving the holy table closer to the people during service time, odd as it seems to us, had the virtue of pointing up the corporate nature of the eucharist and enabling the communicants to participate more effectively in the eucharistic action, both of which are important objectives of the modern Liturgical Movement. Hence it cannot simply be dismissed as a Calvinist aberration!

In colonial America altars were made of wood, in table form, and they were generally smaller (and lower) than the ones advocated by the Victorian Ecclesiologists at a later time. The latter believed that what was correct came from the Middle Ages and embraced the modern concept that the standard height of the altar should be thirty-nine to forty inches, which is a convenient height for a priest of normal size standing before it. The reason why colonial altars were considerably lower is supposed to be a historical accident. During the suppression of Anglicanism under Cromwell, many English people got out of the habit of kneeling in church, and the clergy after the Restoration of 1660 are said to have adopted the unrubrical posture of kneeling before the altar during the consecration, or at least when they received the sacrament, in order to set a good example for their parishioners. To facilitate their handling of the paten and chalice while kneeling, it was expedient to make altars lower than they had been in Archbishop Laud's day or than they would be again under the aegis of the Victorian Ecclesiologists. This swing of the pendulum resulted, of course, in many old altars being replaced by larger ones in the nineteenth century, which explains why very few colonial altars have survived intact, although there are still no fewer than 130 Anglican churches in the United States that were built in the seventeenth and eighteenth centuries.

The use of processional and altar crosses, which have become so much a part of Anglican ceremonial since the Oxford Movement, has a long and involved history. Early Christians emphasized the Resurrection rather than the Crucifixion, and Easter rather than Good Friday set the tone of Sunday worship. In consequence, for the first five centuries or so, there was considerable reluctance to depict the crucifixion of our Lord. Even as late as the fifth-century mosaics at Ravenna, when the cross was used as a Christian symbol, there are no instances of depicting Christ dead upon a cross. Prior to that time our Lord was usually shown as risen rather than dead. He was depicted as Christus Rex, wearing a crown and priestly garments, reigning as prophet, priest, and king. But some of the great heresies of those troublous times fastened on our Lord's divinity and denied his humanity. To counter this view, which would have destroyed the central theological assertions of the faith, the Church began to reassert the humanity of Christ. It did so in two ways:

1. by inserting into the Nicene Creed the phrase "born of the Virgin Mary," which had not been in the original version and
2. by depicting our Lord as dead upon the cross. If he were born of Mary, he was certainly human. And if he died on the cross, he must have been human, for gods don't die, only human beings do.

This was intended to preserve the balance and maintain that our Lord was both divine and human, not one or the other, or in the words of Charles Wesley's Christmas hymn, "Hail th' Incarnate Deity, pleased as man with men to dwell." But it was not until the thirteenth century that the cultus of the passion was greatly developed under the impetus of the Franciscans. Thereafter, realistic crucifixes (i.e., crosses bearing a figure of the crucified Christ) became widespread.

Processional crosses were in use as early as the fourth century, but altar crosses are much later. Medieval altars in England rarely had a cross standing on them. After all, in the Gothic scheme of things the rood screen was the more appropriate location. Besides, early Christian altars had nothing placed on them except what was needed for the celebration of the eucharist. Candles were added, for practical reasons, when olive oil was hard to come by. And in the case of freestanding altars, processional crosses were sometimes placed in a socket behind the altar. But towering crucifixes on a shelf behind the altar belong to the period of the Counter-Reformation.

Some of the late medieval and Renaissance crosses have a figure of Christ on them, but many others do not. Indeed, in the Roman rite, altar crosses were required to bear a figure of Christ no earlier than 1746. Altar crosses were rarely used in post-Reformation English churches until the Oxford Movement, and the few instances known involved private chapels rather than high altars in cathedrals or parish churches. Queen Elizabeth I used one in her Chapel Royal to the consternation of her Puritan subjects. Archbishop Laud and some of his fellow Caroline divines did so in their chapels. But it was the Ritualists and Ecclesiologists who introduced altar crosses and by the end of the nineteenth century succeeded in making them virtually universal in Anglican churches, indeed, so much so that many a church member finds it hard to accept freestanding altars chiefly because they are incompatible with altar crosses that stand directly on the altar. If a cross is to be retained, it may be fastened to the east wall above and behind the celebrant or suspended from the ceiling over the freestanding altar, or the processional cross may be placed in a socket behind the altar as in early medieval times.

In the late nineteenth and early twentieth centuries, when the tendency to copy current Roman Catholic ways was strong, many Anglo-Catholic parishes installed altars fitted with retables or gradines to hold a tabernacle, a cross, and six candlesticks. Sometimes the two candlesticks on the altar itself were designated as the epistle and gospel lights and were lighted only at the eucharist. Other churches, including many Low Church ones, used two seven-branched candlesticks on the retable at morning and evening prayer but not at the eucharist, with the curious result that the medieval, monkish daily offices were dignified with more lights than our

Lord's own service, the eucharist! All this was an innovation, quite alien to Anglican usage, and an inversion of more than a thousand-year tradition of showing greater honor to the Blessed Sacrament. But with the coming of electricity, older forms of illumination, such as candles, became symbols of romantic antiquity in many peoples' minds, and few parish priests were hard put to find donors of seven-branched candelabra.

Against this extravaganza, Percy Dearmer, the Alcuin Club enthusiasts, and the Anglican Society carried on a barrage of rebuttal. They cited long lists of historical documents and argued that the "correct" way, based on English medieval practice, was to have no retable, to use only two candlesticks on the altar itself, and, in addition, to use other lights standing on the pavement near the altar with perhaps two held by carved angels atop riddel posts. It was a question of English medieval Gothic use versus continental baroque practice, and like Tweedledum and Tweedledee, neither was strong enough to carry the day. Some churches favored one and some the other.

When crosses were used in connection with altars, the Anglican Society urged that they depict the risen Lord—Christ in majesty—and not dead upon the cross, because it is the risen Lord with whom we have to do in the eucharist. The afficionadoes of the Society of SS. Peter and Paul, however, favored crucifixes complete with corpus on the grounds that it was only through his sacrificial death that we became reconciled to the all-holy God, and therefore eligible to enter into that relationship that makes Holy Communion a possibility. Needless to say, both views have theological validity, for truth is many faceted, but a single altar cross can represent only one, and not both, of these aspects of the truth.

With the Liturgical Movement came the urge, already described, to make the altar freestanding again, as it had been in the early centuries of Christianity and, experimentally, in the reign of Elizabeth I. This was done, of course, in the interests of making the eucharist more visibly corporate. It had, however, several results that were probably not foreseen. One was that riddel posts, retables, tabernacles, and altar crosses all went by the board, along with the six candlesticks beloved by Anglo-Catholics and seven-branched ones that were dear to the heart of Low Church people. There was, at most, room on the freestanding altar for two candlesticks. The altar cross, if it was to be retained, either had to be removed to the east wall behind the celebrant or replaced by one suspended from the ceiling directly over the altar. Pavement candlesticks could remain but certainly not the row of six candlesticks or the pair of seven-branched ones. If they were retained, they would have to be relegated to a shelf on the reredos well behind the celebrant and altar. Even there they would have to compete for space with flower vases, exiled from the freestanding altar, and perhaps also with the sedilia that in many cases have been relocated in the spot where the altar formerly stood. Tabernacles, of course, are now ecclesiastical "white elephants," and their function is more aesthetically and effectively served by an aumbry or a hanging pyx, as was the case in the Middle Ages before tabernacles came into use.

The altar guild axiom that flowers should never be higher than the altar cross has no basis in documented Anglican history. It is, apparently, a romantic fabrication by well-meaning and devout church people of the late Victorian age. In earlier days, flowers were strewn on the floor, and greens were used in the form of garlands hung on the walls and galleries of the churches, especially at Christmas and Easter, long before altar crosses became virtually an article of faith in Anglican churches in the second half of the nineteenth century.

For the convenience of the church architects and building committees, Dr. Pocknee's *Practical Considerations in the Design of an Altar* are reproduced here:*

> 1. There is no rule, Anglican or Roman, requiring the High altar to be mounted on *three* steps. Much will depend on the size of the sanctuary. Space rather than additional steps should be the primary consideration. The foot-pace on which the altar stands should not be more than 2 feet 9 inches from the front of the altar to the edge of the step, and not less than 2 feet 6 inches.
>
> 2. The riser of any step should not be more than 6 inches, and 5 inches is preferable. Subsidiary steps below the foot-pace are frequently too narrow. Their width should not be less than 22 inches and 25 inches is preferable. Where space allows they should be carried right across the sanctuary rather than returned each side.
>
> 3. If the altar is of stone it should have one slab on top; and it should be one piece of natural stone or marble, not concrete or any artificial composition. The front of the altar should not have detailed carving on it, nor should it be decorated and gilded, so that on the

---

*Cyril E. Pocknee, *The Christian Altar: In History and Today* (London: Mowbray, 1963), 106-107.

last three days of Holy Week when it is exposed it does not present a festive appearance. Wooden altars should also be free of unnecessary carving and decoration.

4. The height of an altar should be 3 feet 3 inches, and not more than 3 feet 5 inches: and it must be wide enough to take a corporal of twenty inches square. It can be wider, but if it is made wider than 3 feet 6 inches there will be difficulties about vesting and clothing the table. The top of the altar should project two or three inches on the side on which the celebrant stands to provide foot room for the feet.

5. Altars should always stand clear of a wall or reredos. This is important for the cleanliness and vesting of the altar. Gradines or shelves are now going out of use everywhere and this is to be commended.

6. Where the conventional type of altar frontal is in use this should not be mounted on a wooden frame, but suspended from an aluminum or brass tube (steel tubing rusts), which is supported by lugs or hooks under the front of the altar. There should be two "frontals" where the altar is visible on both sides. If not, the "throw-over" type of cloth should be used. Over the top of the altar hangs the frontlet (incorrectly called the "super-frontal"). This should not be more than six inches in depth and it should be attached to the coarse linen cloth which covers the top of the altar and hangs some inches down the back. At the back of this cloth there should be an open seam through which a rod may hang to help keep the frontlet and its cloth in position.

7. Altars which have oil or chrism used at their consecration require a wax or cere-cloth to prevent the oil from soiling the fair linen. The fair linen should not merely cover the top of the altar, but hang right down each side to the foot-pace. Nothing is more mean and contrary to the spirit of sound liturgical practice than a fair linencloth which only hangs a few inches over the ends of the altar. Lace and crochet are to be avoided on fair linen. They were quite unknown in the primitive and early medieval period.

8. The canopy, tester or baldaquin should not only cover the area of the altar, but also that of the foot-pace. It will, therefore, be four-square and not oblong in plan.

ALTAR HANGINGS (see also ALTARS)

After the early Church emerged from the age of persecution and became respectable under Constantine, permanent churches were built and provided with holy tables. As a mark of reverence, altars were covered with cloths of costly materials that came down to the floor on all four sides, for it was the place where the faithful experienced the presence of the risen Lord. In later centuries this "pall," as it was called, was decorated with embroidered symbols and sometimes with jewels. Over the carpet a fair linen cloth was spread, usually at the time of the offertory. Thus arrayed, the altar was considered the most sacred object in the church—other than the blessed sacrament itself—and was held in Christian piety to be none other than the throne of God on earth.

Later, in the course of the Middle Ages, the carpet was pared down and fitted to the altar and so became the frontal of received tradition. By that time altars were no longer freestanding but placed against the east wall, and their ends were usually obscured by riddel curtains. Hence, what was the pall or throw was now merely a cloth hung to cover the front of the altar. Sometimes it was suspended by rings from underneath the slightly projecting mensa, or altar top. In that case, a second cloth, also of silk or damask, called a frontlet, was hung over the upper six or eight inches of the frontal in order to conceal the means by which the latter was suspended. If no carved reredos was behind the altar, another cloth of rich material was hung there, usually from a rod connecting the top of the two rear riddel posts. This hanging, called a dorsal or dossal, served as a reredos and was usually the same depth as the frontal, i.e., about forty inches. (Note: It was sometimes called a superfrontal. In modern times this word has erroneously been applied to the frontlet.)

The Caroline divines revived the early Christian type of altar cloth in the seventeenth century, and it is known today as a "Laudian" or "Jacobean" frontal. Despite that name, it was not peculiar to English churches and was in use in various parts of the continent, including Spain. In England and America it survived, along with fitted frontals, until the nineteenth century when the Ecclesiologists ruled it out in favor of the latter, for they perceived that the fitted frontal was in vogue in the thirteenth century, and that constituted the golden age that provided them with their notion of what alone was correct for Anglican use.

In the case of altar hangings, as in other things, the pendulum of fashion has swung to and fro several times in the last thousand years. With the coming of freestanding altars in our own day, there has been a widespread revival of the Laudian or Jacobean altar cloth. If there is enough space around the freestanding altar, this type of frontal can be enormously effective. It lends itself to new materials and designs and is appropriate to contemporary churches. It has the great advantage of requiring no hanging devices and therefore needs no frontlet. One of its drawbacks from a practical view is that unless modified, the corners project far out, thus taking a lot of space and threatening to trip up absentminded priests as well as ill-at-ease acolytes. Also, the heavy brocades and damask on top of the altar may make a tall and top-heavy chalice easy to knock over. And they present harder problems of storage than do fitted frontals. But a good ecclesiastical supply house can easily be prevailed upon to modify the corners, substitute a thinner cloth to cover the top of the altar, and devise snaps or grippers so that the frontal can be flattened for convenient storage when not in use.

The decoration on frontals, whether Laudian or fitted, has changed considerably over the centuries. The frontals used in colonial days, like those in the Middle Ages, relied for their decoration largely upon the texture and color of the rich materials of which they were made. Velvet and silk were much in vogue in the eighteenth century, and frontals made of them were further embellished with the use of gold or silver fringe. Not much of a color sequence was preserved in colonial America, although we have documentary evidence of frontals of crimson, purple, green, and of at least one pulpit fall of cloth of gold. Crimson velvet was by far the most common, fringed with gold or silver and, sometimes in wealthy churches, with gold embroidered symbols such as a tetragrammaton (i.e., the four Hebrew letters that formed the name of God transliterated by modern scholars as Yahweh) or IHS (a monogram for the name Jesus) surrounded by a "glory" (i.e., rays emanating from a center focus like the shining of the sun or a star). Probably the average parish church used its newest and best frontal, regardless of its color, on great feasts like Christmas, Easter, and Whitsunday, its old and slightly worn one on ferial occasions, and black for Lent and burials. The *Virginia Gazette* in 1770 gave this account of the funeral of the royal governor, Lord Botetourt, in Bruton Parish Church, Williamsburg: "At the western gate the corpse was removed from the hearse, and, carried by eight bearers, the Gentlemen appointed supporting the pall, placed in the centre of the church, on a carpet of black. The altar, pulpit, and his Excellency's seat, were likewise hung with black."

Kneeling cushions at the altar rail today are often made of needlepoint. There is no known evidence that such was the case in times past. Modern liturgical experts are distinctly lukewarm about kneelers decorated with needlepoint, and they recommend that the time and effort required for making them be devoted instead to producing handsome frontals, vestments, and banners or, perhaps, cushions for the altar and sedilia. These, they maintain, are more directly related to worship and less likely to be a distraction to the worshiper. If, however, a church wishes to make needlepoint kneelers today, it would be desirable to use designs appropriate to the time when the church was built. For example, an eighteenth-century church should have kneelers with curvilinear designs taken from nature, such as vines with bunches of grapes, sheaves of wheat, and flowers, whereas a Victorian church of the Gothic Revival might look better with the kinds of designs that were favored by the Ecclesiologists or that are taken from illuminated manuscripts of medieval origin. The Victorians delighted in crosses, "Chi-Rhos," and other arbitrary rather than natural symbols.

Care should be taken when trying to use modern designs in churches built in bygone styles. It is recommended that advice be sought from architects, artists, and other competent consultants before giving the signal to willing needleworkers to proceed. Mixing periods and styles can be tastefully done, but without good advice it can produce a discordant decor that is aesthetically disastrous. And if it is artistically hazardous to thrust contemporary hangings and vestments into churches of antiquated design, the reverse is equally perilous. Imagine an altar and a priest vested in the high baroque style of the Society of SS. Peter and Paul in a church of avant garde design! Instead of new wine in old skins, it would be a case of old wine in new skins! The same, of course, applies to crosses, candlesticks, communion vessels, banners, stained-glass windows, and virtually everything else.

The remaining object used on the altar, other than the communion plate, is, of course, the missal stand. The prevailing type, a stand made of brass with varying degrees of Gothic Revival decoration, was pushed by the Ecclesiologists. It can be said to be appropriate, if at all, in a Victorian Gothic church. But a church of Georgian or of contemporary design should avoid using a period piece that belongs to the late nineteenth and early twentieth centuries. Two centuries and more ago, the practice was to place on the altar a cushion covered with rich damask or brocade and embellished with silk tassels to accommodate the celebrant's Prayer Book. This type or, failing that, a missal stand made of walnut looks better and is more appropriate, particularly on altars that are vested with a Laudian frontal. It is soft to the touch, more colorful to the eye, and blends with the overall decor.

The common color sequence of altar hanging and vestments, the white, red, purple, and green sequence, was taken over from the Roman usage in the nineteenth century. Despite its lack of antiquity and its recent appearance in Anglican churches, it has much to recommend it. For one thing, it is well known and widely used. For another, in this day of ecumenical rapprochement it represents one more bond between separated communions. But the Alcuin Club–Dearmer–Anglican Society axis succeeded in modifying it in English cathedrals (and many parish churches) by reviving the medieval use of a "lenten array," unbleached linen hangings stencilled in black and blood red with symbols of our Lord's Passion from Ash Wednesday until Palm Sunday and dark red linen hangings for Holy Week through Maundy Thursday. Hangings of purple silk or velvet, despite their somber color, are too rich for Lent. Unbleached linen, on the other hand, is austere without being gloomy and therefore is more appropriate to the liturgical function of Lent.

Another variation that has won some parishes to it is the use of a three-color sequence: white for feasts of our Lord (and for baptisms, weddings, and burials); blue for solemn occasions such as Advent and Lent; and red for Pentecost, martyrs' days, and for ferial occasions. This red-white-and-blue sequence, by eliminating one color, costs less, hence it is desirable for new churches and for older churches that have just replaced an old altar with a new one of a different size. As time goes on and would-be donors appear, green hangings can always be added and, if more memorials are wanted, purple or a lenten array as well. The original blue hangings can then be used for Advent.

BURIALS and COLUMBARIA

Throughout the history of the Church, Christian burial rites have expressed concern for the bereaved, hope for the departed, belief in the resurrection, and reverence for the body as sharing in the resurrection. The rite in early Christian days consisted of five elements: (1) prayer in the house while the body was prepared for burial; (2) a procession to the church with white vestments, psalms of hope, and alleluias of victory, expressing the conviction that in Christ we triumph over eternal death; (3) a short service of praise and thanksgiving in the presence of the body; (4) a eucharist in the parish church expressing belief in the relationship that still exists between the faithful, living and dead, symbolized by the kiss of peace given to the corpse; and (5) interment with the body placed with feet towards the east as a sign of hope of the Second Coming of Christ, which according to Matthew 24:27 will be from the east, i.e., "For as the lightning comes from the east and shines as far as the west, so will be the coming of the Son of man."

During the Middle Ages, when people were obsessed with the idea of sin and damnation, the burial office was shorn of much of its resurrection joy. Instead, it came to be habited in somber garments suggestive of sorrow and dread. Most of the five elements were retained, but the emphasis was shifted to bring the rite into line with the theory of purgatory. And, appropriately enough, the liturgical color was changed from white to violet or black. The funeral began as the somber procession bearing the body reached the entrance of the churchyard. A roofed structure called a "lych-gate" (from the Anglo-Saxon word for a corpse) protected the body and its bearers from the elements until met by the priest and his attendants for reception into the church. A few lych-gates have survived in England, and a few have been built in America as a result of the Victorian enchantment with things medieval. If you have one, by all means preserve it, for they are period pieces and nowadays few and far between!

As the funeral proceeded, the corpse was carried into the church and placed, often on a carpet, at the head of the nave before the rood screen with it great crucifix symbolizing the fact that our Lord's sacrifical death alone makes it possible for the penitent faithful to enter paradise. But medieval theology had both liturgical and architectural consequences. It emphasized the concept of purgatory, which has been defined as "the place or state of temporal punishment, where those who have died in the grace of God are expiating their venial fruits and such pains as are still due to forgiven mortal sins, before being admitted to the Beatific Vision."* It was to shorten the time in purgatory that chantry endowments for daily votive masses came into existence, and by the end of the Middle Ages most churches were cluttered with such chantry chapels. The sixteenth century reformers swept all this away and reaffirmed the belief that the dead slept in peace until the Parousia and the great day of judgement. Archbishop Cranmer accordingly eliminated all references to purgatory in the Prayer Book and

---

*See under "Purgatory" in F. L. Cross, ed. *The Oxford Dictionary Of The Christian Church*, London: Oxford University Press, 1957, 1125.

shifted the emphasis to rest in Christ and the ultimate resurrection to life eternal. But he did not go the whole way towards early Christian joy in connection with the faithful departed. Perhaps because of his conservatism or because of strong Calvinist opposition to prayers for the departed, he retained only cautiously worded petitions for the dead and shrank from declaring unequivocally that the deceased was forthwith delivered from suffering. Even these watered-down petitions were dropped in the 1552 Prayer Book, and specific prayers for the departed were not reintroduced into any Anglican rite until the appearance of the 1637 Scottish Prayer Book under the influence of the Caroline divines whose theological views were shared by some of the Scottish bishops.

Although prayer for the dead was conspiciously absent from the Prayer Book in both England and the United States until comparatively recent times, the practice of praying for them continued and was even enjoined by ecclesiastical authority. The "bidding prayer" prescribed by the fifty-fifth of the canons of 1604 to be used before sermons included these words: "Ye shall pray for Christ's holy Catholike Church . . . and for all those which are departed out of this life in the Faith of Christ and pray unto God that we may have grace to direct our lives after their good example: that this life ended, we may be made partakers with them of the glorious Resurrection in the Life Everlasting." Popular use of prayer for the dead can also be seen in epitaphs, books of devotion that were widely used, and in the opinions of pious writers of repute.

The burial rite used in eighteenth-century America was that of the 1662 English Prayer Book and was very much like every American Prayer Book from 1789 through 1928. Read attentively, it gave ample evidence of hope, particularly in the appointed lessons and in the words of committal ("In sure and certain hope of the Resurrection to eternal life through our Lord Jesus Christ") and in the prayer ("Almighty God with whom do live the spirits of those who depart hence in the Lord, and with whom the souls of the faithful, after they are delivered from the burden of the flesh, are in joy and felicity"). But the ceremonial that usually accompanied these exhilarating assertions of hope, at least until recent years, often obscured the joy. It was partly, perhaps, the lingering effect of the received medieval tradition and partly the continuing influence of the Calvinistic approach to death, which, thanks to predestination, meant that, like Russian roulette, there was a good chance that in any particular case the deceased would not make it to eternal bliss.

Despite the comforting words of the Bible, the Prayer Book, and the hymns, the burial of the dead was too frequently given ceremonial trappings—black hangings and vestments—that tended to negate the tone of the rite. Also, with the growth of population and the apostasy of many Americans from active church participation, funeral parlors have become the frequent locale for burial rites that priests are called to take. And in many cases the funeral directors either play down the reality of death or otherwise create an atmosphere that does little to manifest the joy of Christian hope. On that account, experience shows that for the faithful departed, at least, the parish church with it familiar symbols and associations is by far the more appropriate place for the burial office.

One of the great changes that has come about in our century is the liturgical recovery of more of the early Christian hope and joy by having the service in church, by joining it with a eucharist for the departed, and by using white vestments, hangings, and pall together with Easter hymns. All these bring the ceremonial, including the setting of worship, into focus with the inspiring and uplifting words of the rite, and that should be the "object all sublime" of all parish priests, who, after all, bear a heavy responsibility in Anglican canon law and tradition for ordering all services in conformity to the doctrine, discipline, and worship of the Church.

Another notable change has been the growth of the practice of cremation in this century. Until the late nineteenth century, most parish churches, other than some urban ones, had churchyards. After the burial order had been recited in church, the committal took place almost in the shadow of the church's walls. As churchyards filled up and population ballooned, cemeteries at a distance from, and often unconnected with, the church became the usual place of burial. In recent years these, in turn, have for practical reasons given way, more and more, to crematoria. Since cremated remains occupy much less space than embalmed corpses and offer no threat to the public health of the community, it has become practical once again to have the interment of human remains in and around parish churches, even those in cities, for small plots of land or unused portions of crypts can inexpensively be fitted to hold the ashes of many of the departed. These "columbaria," as they are called, reduce the pressure on overcrowded public cemeteries, cost less than a plot, and have the inestimable advantage of locating the remains of the faithful departed in or near the church rather than in an indiscriminate assemblage of dead bodies in a public or commercially owned cemetery far removed from the sacred edifice hallowed by personal and family associations and by uninterrupted offerings of prayer, praise, word, and sacraments.

To meet the 1979 Prayer Book requirements for burial, a church should have ample space at the head of the nave to accommodate a casket, a pall of white (or some other appropriate color), and a paschal candlestick and candle to place near it. Other standing candlesticks called "hearse lights"—usually six in number—were used in the Middle Ages, revived by the Victorian Ecclesiologists, and endorsed by both Percy Dearmer and the Society of SS. Peter and Paul. Such consensus about nonessential ceremonial detail is rare and constitutes a recommendation to use them. The hearse lights, however, should be in a style appropriate to that of the church: Gothic in Gothic Revival churches, baroque in churches of that style, and contemporary in modern churches.

CHANCEL SCREENS

Derived from the Latin *cancellus* or "bar of latticework," the chancel was originally the screen that separated the part of a church that was reserved for the clergy from the nave. Later the word was used for the part that was east of the screen. By the late Middle Ages, the chancel was recognized as consisting of two subdivisions: (1) the choir and (2) the sanctuary, or area around the high altar. The screen that divided the chancel from the nave eventually became more ornate and was often made of stone. In medieval teaching, the nave represented the world, "the Church militant," and the chancel stood for paradise. As the only way one could enter paradise was through the sacrificial death of our Lord, a large crucifix depicting the dead Christ was commonly erected upon the chancel screen, which came to be known as the "rood screen" from the Anglo-Saxon word for a cross.

With the coming of the Reformation and in insistence that the liturgy be in the vernacular so that the people could participate in it, there was a Protestant tendency on the continent to remove rood screens in order to reduce two-room churches into one-room ones thereby making them auditory, i.e., designed to promote the hearing of the liturgy by all present. Later, when the Counter-Reformation entered its baroque phase, many rood screens were removed from Roman Catholic churches in order to make way for the "dramatic" altar with its towering and ornate reredos. The Counter-Reformation favored the visual over the audio aspects of worship, and the medieval rood screens got in the way and prevented their magnificent altars from visually dominating church interiors. It was only in England that most of the medieval screens survived and even there more or less by accident. The extreme reformers in Edward VI's day, it is true, pulled down many of the roods or crucifixes under the impression that they represented popish superstition. But that orgy of destruction was stopped by Queen Mary's accession in 1553, and screens were further reprieved from the vandal's axe by an order of Elizabeth I in 1561 decreeing their retention. A majority of them survived, it is said, until the nineteenth century when many of them fell victim to well-meaning but ill-informed church restorers of Victorian days.

The building of chancel screens was not confined to pre-Reformation times. A number were built under Laudian influence in the reign of Charles I. Bishops often asked questions about them in their visitation articles. The bishop of Norwich, for example, asked each priest in his diocese in 1638: "Is your chancel divided from the nave or body of the church, with a partition of stone, boards, wainscot, grates, or otherwise? Wherein is there a decent strong door to open and shut (as occasion serveth), with lock and key, to keep out boys, girls, or irreverent men and women? And are dogs kept from coming to despoil or profane the Lord's table?"* Puritans, dogs, and unruly children seem to have given the Caroline divines a lot of trouble! Later, when altar rails became the norm, the chancel screen with its locked door was no longer needed to keep the altar from being profaned.

One screen that was erected in an English church by a private donor in 1640 was described as being adorned "with curiously carved woodwork" depicting instruments of our Lord's Passion, including not only those directly connected with the crucifixion but also such things as torches, lanterns, and sword of St. Peter, the ear of Malchus, the cock, and the pillar and scourges. Although chancel screens were retained and new ones built, they were generally not solid but open so that the eucharistic action in the chancel could be seen and the priest heard by the worshipers in the nave.

Colonial churches were simplified copies of English parish churches. The earliest ones in Virginia were simple, half-timbered, thatched structures like the first four Jamestown churches. Although common in the seventeenth century, none has survived.

---

*Vernon Staley, ed. *Hierurgia Anglicana,* Part I, London: De La More Press, 1902, 19-20.

43

Next came brick churches of which St. Luke's, Isle of Wight County, and the tower of the fifth Jamestown church alone survive. They represent the last of the Elizabethan phase of Gothic architecture but with some evidences of the dawn of Renaissance influence. The second Bruton Parish Church (1683) and St. Peter's, New Kent (1703), with their curvilinear gables reflect the Jacobean phase. Merchants Hope Church (1657) and most eighteenth century churches are examples of Georgian style. Those who are acquainted with English examples of these styles will perceive a time lag of a generation or more between the mother country and the Old Dominion. It may have been the result of nostalgia. An Englishman in seventeenth century Virginia, remembering his parish church at home, may have chosen to build a church in the colony modeled after an older one in England rather than opt for the current style in use in the mother country.

Following English practice, the early Virginians commonly provided their little churches in the wilderness with simple chancel screens. Not a single example has survived, but the following churches are known from vestry records to have had chancel screens:

Middle Plantation Church, 1660
Christ Church, Middlesex County, 1665
Lancaster Parish Church,
    Middlesex County, 1667
Poplar Springs Church,
    Petsworth Parish, Gloucester, 1677
The three churches of Christ Church Parish,
    Middlesex, that were ordered built in 1710
Trinity Church, Portsmouth, 1764

In addition, it is possible, even probable, that the "Chancell of Cedar" in the 1610 Jamestown church was a chancel screen.

The 1660 Middle Plantation Church seems to have set the style for the later ones, because the churches of Christ Church and Lancaster parishes were ordered built "according to the Modell of the Middle Plantation Church in all respects." And a description of a chancel screen appears in the specifications for Poplar Spring Church in 1677; "the Chancell to be 15 foote and a Screen to be runn a Crosse the church with ballisters." We can, therefore, visualize it as a simplified version of an English architectural builder's book with an account of a chancel screen as "close paneling beneath about three feet to three feet six inches high, on which stands screen work composed of slender turned ballusters or regular wooden mullions, supporting tracery . . . with cornices, cresting, etc., and often painted in brilliant colors or gilded." The three churches of Christ Church Parish, Middlesex, ordered built in 1710 were to be furnished with "a commendable [i.e., handsome or ornate] Screene to divide the Church from the Chancell," and the last mention of a chancel screen in the vestry book of the parish was in 1715. Although we have no account of the construction of chancel screens in Virginia after that date, we know that Trinity Church, Portsmouth, built in 1764 had one, because a French visitor in 1794 mentioned its "rood screen" in recording his impression of the interior. They were still being built in England in the eighteenth century and were probably more common in America than has been realized.

Colonial churches that did not have chancel screens nonetheless maintained the liturgical distinction between chancel and nave by reading matins, the litany, and antecommunion in the nave and celebrating the eucharist at the altar that was construed to be the chancel. This distinction was given architectural recognition in many churches—especially those built before 1750—by placing a six-inch step in the center aisle where a rood screen would normally have been in days gone by. In 1712, for example, the vestry of Christ Church Parish, Middlesex County, Virginia, specified in connection with the three new churches that were being built for the parish "that the Chancell be raised one step [six-inches] higher than the said church floore," and Bruton Parish Church, Williamsburg, built 1710–15, has a similar step but no chancel screen.

The use of chancel screens declined after 1715 and went out of fashion by the Revolution. Indeed, many existing ones were removed by the Evangelicals and other church people who favored churches with no central aisle, with pulpit, altar, and font together rather than as three distinct liturgical centers. But the tide receded after the first quarter of the nineteenth century, and ecclesiastical architecture was soon engulfed by the rising Ecclesiologists. With the Romantic Movement, the popular novels of Sir Walter Scott, and the Gothic Revival in architecture, medieval ways became more attractive than they had been in the previous century when supporters of the Age of Reason deplored Gothic as a barbarous relic of a superstitious age.

By the end of Victoria's eventful reign, chancel screens by the dozen had made their appearance in American churches, thanks to the temper of the age and to such architects as Henry Vaughan, Ralph Adams Cram, and Bertram Goodhue. But the triumphal return of the chancel screen proved to be of no long continuance. The twentieth century witnessed the rise of the Liturgical Movement, which, by emphasizing the corporate nature of the eucharist, instilled an aversion to chancel screens as something that stood between the celebrant and the people and, therefore symbolized what was wrong with the received tradition of the setting of worship. Like the church people of a century and more earlier, the advocates of the Liturgical Movement preferred the one-room concept of a church, and chancel screens by their nature divided churches into two. In consequence, many chancel screens were demolished in the interest of giving architectural expression to emphasis upon the corporate nature of the eucharist.

In cases where the chancel screen was retained, the symbolic difficulty it presented was obviated by setting up a nave altar to be used at large services. In such instances, the chancel screen acquired a new lease on life by being converted functionally into a reredos for the nave altar as it had been occasionally in the Middle Ages. This device preserved existing screens, yet accomplished its objective by adding another altar rather than by subtracting a chancel screen. The old high altar, moreover, did not have to be replaced or moved (which is costly in the case of stone altars), and the chancel could serve as a chapel for weekday services.

If you have a handsome chancel screen in your church, you would be well advised to retain it, and if you have a handsome high altar, save it. It is quite possible, in most cases, to meet the needs of current liturgical practice without destroying good examples of such furnishings. Given the kaleidoscopic rearrangement of the setting of worship in order to accommodate liturgical change, it may well be that what you have from the past will once again be valued and useful. Hence, the axiom in such cases should be the following: "If it is of good materials and design, preserve it."

COMMUNION VESSELS

Although strictly speaking not architectural, communion vessels and the bread of the eucharist are an essential part of the material setting of worship.

The vessel used by our Lord at the institution of the eucharist, known in song and story as the Holy Grail, was probably an ordinary two-handled cup of that period. Similar vessels were frequently used during the age of persecution when Christians met in private homes for the breaking of bread each Lord's Day. After the recognition of Christianity by Constantine, the Church emerged from the shadows and erected permanent buildings to house its worship. And as it grew in numbers and in wealth, the Church began to acquire communion vessels more skillfully made and of finer materials. Chalices of precious metals, of hollowed out sardonyx, and of glass appeared and became increasingly common. Simpler vessels were used by missionaries such as St. Boniface and by the early monastic communities that practiced asceticism. But as time went on, more and more chalices and patens were of gold and silver.

For the first thousand years of the Church's history, the laity as well as the clergy partook of the chalice as well as the paten. The celebrant consecrated wine in a small chalice, which after the clergy had received was poured into much larger ones already containing wine, for it was believed that a small amount of consecrated wine was capable of extending the virtue of the consecration to the entire contents of the larger vessel. These larger ones, known as "ministerial chalices," usually had two handles for the convenience of the deacons who carried them, and the people were communicated from them.

About the twelfth century, however, the chalice was withdrawn from the laity, and the large ministerial chalices went out of use. Thereafter only the clergy received in both kinds. Hence, chalices made after that time, although of silver gilt and gold encrusted with precious stones, required only very small bowls and no handles. By then chalices were made in the form with which we are familiar—thanks to Victorian Ecclesiologists—consisting of a bowl, knop, and foot. More or less the same was true to the paten. There was a small "consecration paten" designed to go with the chalice, one or more ciboria to hold additional bread, and extra ministerial patens to facilitate the communion.

An unusual feature of receiving communion in the early centuries when the people still shared the consecrated wine was the use of a "fistula" or "pipa" or "calamus"—names applied to a silver or gold tube, like a modern straw, through which the communicant sucked consecrated wine from the chalice. Presumably this enabled our Dark Age and early medieval forebears to be communicated without getting their beards in the sacred species! Who would have thought that the coming of beards into general use so different from the fashion of the first-century Greeks and Romans, would have brought about such drastic changes in the physical aspects of Holy Communion?

One of the "objects all sublime" of the sixteenth-century

reformers was to restore the chalice to the laity. When that change took place, the late medieval chalices proved to be much too small. To meet the need of this liturgical change, the Church replaced its inherited chalices with much larger ones, and churchwarden accounts thereafter distinguished the new ones from the old by such adjectives as "fayre," "decent," and "comely." The common form used after the accession of Edward VI, except during Queen Mary's reign, was copied from German originals, but in some instances a pre-Reformation foot and knop were brazed to a new and larger cup.

The Puritan-minded clergy, in order to point up the common meal aspect of the Lord's Supper, were prone to use secular winecups and beakers for the eucharist. Against this trend there was a reaction under the first two Stuart kings led by the Catholic-minded clergy. As a result, James Gilchrist, in his *Anglican Church Plate,* has identified over seventy neo-Gothic chalices, most of them of great beauty, that were made during the High Church revival of Andrewes and Laud. Even so, the general run of new church plate was undistinguished and resembled the secular cups of the day, although of silver or silver gilt. Some of them, however, are examples of skilled craft.

By the eighteenth century most Anglican chalices were variations of the beaker shape with a stem and a round base. The patens, too, were often footed and made, when inverted, to serve as covers for the chalices. The foot was convenient for removing the paten from the chalice and for holding it while ministering the bread. Such chalices were quite large by both medieval and modern standards. The Jamestown chalice of 1660, for example, is ten and five-eighths inches tall, and the 1750 chalice of Accomack Parish, Virginia, is eleven inches in height. Communion sets almost always included a large sliver flagon, for in colonial days communicants took more than a mere sip from the chalice. And because the Caroline divines placed great emphasis on the self-offering of the faithful to God in thanksgiving for our Lord's oblation for the sins of the world, the alms basin took a great symbolic value. Almost always of sterling silver and accounted as part and parcel of the communion plate, alms basins were commonly placed upright at the rear of the altar where we would expect to find an altar cross.

Until the Industrial Revolution with its ability to mass produce and lower the unit cost of items, Anglican communion plate was of gold, silver gilt, or sterling silver, the last mentioned being almost universal in colonial America. New churches in remote locations, especially after the Revolution, may have used pewter vessels as a temporary makeshift until they could procure silver ones. But in general anything less than pure silver was regarded as unworthy of a decent and proper worship of almighty God, the Kings of kings and Lord of lords.

Needless to say, with the advent of the Ritualists and Ecclesiologists, the medieval form of the chalice and paten returned and almost completely displaced the larger communion vessels that had sufficed for nearly three centuries. Some High Church people were so enthusiastic about their neo-Gothic plate that they vied with one another to see who could fit the largest number of jewels or the most enamel decoration on their chalices. Many a devout Anglo-Catholic laywoman bequeathed her heirloom jewelry for this purpose. By Edwardian days, some art nouveau jewelers went in for designing altar ware in a modern style, and some notable examples appeared. Meanwhile, the church supply houses continued to turn out inexpensive chalices and patens along the lines of nineteenth-century taste. In the period between World War I and II when the High Church party was riding high, many churches were beautified and enriched with fine plate. But Anglo-Catholics fell into two camps: those who were content to follow Roman Catholic taste and those who urged the recovery of English medieval usage. Silversmiths were obliged, therefore, to produce plate in the baroque style for the Roman buffs and in the Gothic style for the Sarum party. In neither case could they develop an indigenous, contemporary Anglican style. That remained until after World War II, when a great variety of modern designs appeared, and chalices and patens were made of ceramics, glass, pewter, and stainless steel, as well as of silver and silver gilt. Modern pewter, now no longer cheap, is a magnificent metal alloy, and stainless steel has enough practical virtues to recommend it to any priest who is bold enough to reject the principle that nothing should ever be done for the first time!

The early Christians used leavened bread for the eucharist as the Eastern Orthodox churches still do. But the medieval Latin church found wafer bread more practical, and its use became universal in the West. The 1549 Prayer Book, endorsing the received tradition, required the use of wafer bread "unleavened and round" for the mass. Reforming influence, with its emphasis on scriptural authority even for details of worship, urged a change. Accordingly, the 1552 Prayer Book made concessions. While not forbidding the older practice, it declared that "it shall suffice that the Bread be such as is usual to be eaten." In other words, wafer bread is normal, but leavened bread may be used—a characteristically Anglican solution to a controversy that involves no principle! Within a generation, however, the use of "the best wheaten bread," i.e., leavened bread, became increasingly popular and by the eighteenth century was virtually universal in England and remained so until the Ritualists succeeded in reversing the custom there and throughout the Anglican Communion. In recent decades, however, the Liturgical Movement has generated a renewed desire to use leavened bread because of the valuable symbolism in all sharing one bread, as they do one chalice. It also makes the "fraction," the third coordinate part of the four-action eucharist, a practical necessity rather than a vestigial, symbolic ceremony in preparation for Holy Communion. The seesaw between the two kinds of bread has spanned a thousand years of Church history, and, unless the compromise principle of the 1552 Prayer Book continues indefinitely, the seesaw may well continue for centuries to come. What is unbroken practice since apostolic days is the use of bread, not the form of the bread used. Leavened bread as used by the Orthodox church from the beginning or wafer bread as used in the Western medieval tradition is, and has been, capable of being changed by proper ecclesiastical authority. Perhaps this, too, can be described in the words of Queen Elizabeth, used in connection with the proper location of the altar: "There seemeth no matter of great moment . . . saving for uniformity."

The use of leavened bread has certain liturgical ramifications: it requires much larger patens and ciboria than would serve for wafer bread, and by making more crumbs it requires more careful handling by the priest and the communicants in order to avoid irreverence. Perhaps we shall need larger linen corporals, which in turn will require larger altars. We may even have to revive the use of "houseling cloths," a long, narrow linen cloth used at the eucharist in the later Middle Ages and well into the eighteenth century. It was spread or held before the communicants at the time of receiving the sacrament in order to prevent any dropping or spilling of the sacred elements. J. Wickham Legg in his *English Church Life from the Restoration to the Tractarian Movement* (London: 1914) cites the fact that a housling cloth was held in front of every English sovereign (except James II, who as a Roman Catholic declined to receive the sacrament) at his or her coronation from Charles II to George IV and names various English parishes that have afforded it unbroken use.

CREDENCE TABLES

Medieval churches usually had stone altars and credences (which are shelves or tables near the altar to hold bread and wine needed for the offertory) and also a lavabo bowl, towel, and a container for water. In the days of Edward VI, when the duke of Northumberland was pillaging English churches, credences as well as stone altars were systematically destroyed. But they reappeared in the mini-Catholic Revival under the Caroline divines, as we know from contemporary descriptions of church interiors in the reign of Charles I. Canterbury Cathedral, for example, was described in 1635 as having "a credentia or side table, with a bason and ewer on napkins, and a towel to wash before the consecration", and one of the charges leveled by the disgruntled Purtians against Archbishop Laud in 1641 was that in his chapel he had "a credentia or side table . . . on which the elements were to be placed on a clean linen cloth before they were brought to the altar to be consecrated."*

Needless to say, the Laudian altars and credence tables were rooted out of English churches under the aegis of the Lord Protector, Oliver Cromwell, in the 1650s. Although most things were changed back after the Restoration of Charles II in 1660, we hear little of credence tables for the next two centuries or so. Perhaps the liturgical practice of the time was sufficiently different from that of Laud's day so as to render them unnecessary. If so, one can only wonder where the bread and wine were kept prior to their being placed on the altar at the offertory! In any event, the crowded little sanctuaries of most colonial churches afforded little space for such pieces of furniture. After the Revolution, the Evangelicals had no patience with what they considered to be medieval and therefore "popish."

The revival of credence tables came about after the Ecclesiologists —in the 1840s—set about to restore the medieval arrangement of church interiors. Included in this package were both the stone altar and the credence table of stone or wood. Predictably, both were perceived as medieval, and both incited the Evangelicals to wrath.

---

*Vernon Staley, ed. *Hierurgia Anglicana,* Part I London: Da La More Press, 1902, 78, 91

When the late eleventh-century Church of the Holy Sepulchre (also known locally as the Round Church) in Cambridge was restored in the early 1840s, a stone altar and a credence were installed. The incumbent, however, did not approve of what the churchwardens had done on the advice of the architect, and he inveighed against the "Stone altar . . . [and] the Popish accompaniment of a Credence Table." A legal battle ensued, resulting in the consistory court of the diocese upholding the legality of the stone altar and granting an additional faculty (i.e., license) for the credence table. Undismayed and determined "to use every means to remove these abominable pieces of superstition and Popery from my Church," the vicar appealed the case to the province of Canterbury's court of arches, which reversed the lower court's decision on the grounds that since a stone altar could not be moved, it was not a communion table "within the meaning of the Rubric" of the 1662 Prayer Book and "that the Credence Table being an adjunct, must follow its principal."*

The Cambridge Camden Society derided the court's decision and heaped scorn upon the vicar and the judges for the stress "laid upon the use of stone in this question, as if wood were essentially Protestant, and stone essentially Popish." The controversy dragged on and became too involved to chronicle briefly. It did, however, foster the idea that the agenda of the proponents of the Oxford Movement (or Tractarians) and of the Cambridge Ecclesiologists were but two sides of the same coin. Or, as one opponent put it, "as Romanism is taught *Analytically* at Oxford, it is taught *Artistically* at Cambridge—that it is inculcated theoretically, in tracts, at one university, and it is sculptured, painted, and graven at the other . . . in a word, that the *'Ecclesiologist'* of Cambridge is identical in doctrine with the Oxford *Tracts for the Times.'*

In rebuttal, the spokespersons for the Ecclesiologists, instead of denying the charge that the Cambridge Camden Society had a definite theological position, merely quibbled about the accuracy of some of the details cited by their antagonists and stressed the fact that many items to which the Evangelicals took exception as "popish inventions" were in use in the Church of England after the Reformation. They chose to ignore the fact that some of them,

*James F. White, *The Cambridge Movement*, Cambridge: The University Press, 1962, 137-8, 142.

such as the credence table, almost completely disappeared from English churches for nearly two hundred years.

Despite adverse court decisions and popular revulsions whipped up by their opponents, the Ecclesiologists held their ground and in the course of time carried the day. Most of the things they advocated were eventually accepted and became familiar objects in Anglican churches everywhere. Today scarcely a church lacks a credence table, for example, or would decline to accept the offer of one as a memorial. Indeed, it is hard to imagine that anyone could have thought such an innocuous and useful piece of furniture as a credence table to be an object of superstition or a symbol of popery when in truth it is an inheritance from the medieval church, shared alike by Rome and Canterbury.

Marion Hatchett, in the article already cited, has this advice for architects, priests, and building committees:

> The credence should be convenient to the altar but unobtrusive. It should be large enough to accommodate all the vessels and linens needed at the largest services, as well as the altar books and offering plates. If ablutions are done in the chancel, the credence should be large enough to serve this purpose as well.

A liturgical practice that has become widespread in recent decades is the offertory procession, and this has created the need for an additional credence table at the rear of the church to hold the eucharistic elements until the offertory. At that point the ushers carry them, along with the alms and other offerings, forward to the chancel and present them to the celebrant. This credence should be large enough to hold the containers for the bread and wine and for the offering plates. If it is placed in the center aisle, it should be small enough not to be in the way of worshipers entering the church or of the choir procession. If the aisle is too narrow or the credence too large, it is wiser to locate the table elsewhere than in the center aisle.

FLAGS

Visitors to English churches often see tattered flags hanging high up in the nave and transepts, and those from America are often surprised to learn that it is the custom to consign old regimental and other service flags there in preference to burning them. This custom has not caught on in the United States, although there is a widespread feeling that no church is properly furnished unless it has an American and an Episcopal church flag permanently

53

displayed in it. Some would add their state flag as well. But Americans cannot bear to see flags gradually disintegrate, as is the case with old battle flags in British churches. As soon as one of our flags fade or shows signs of becoming threadbare, some patriotic parishioner is almost certain to offer to replace it and reverently consign the old one to the flames. Perhaps it is time to reconsider and even follow the English precedent. Hanging old and revered flags up between the rafters has much to recommend it, not least because it lends a note of color where it is usually much needed. And in that location such flags are far enough from the floor so that the worshiper is not painfully aware of their gradual disintegration over the years.

A word needs to be said about the proper placement of flags in church, and especially of "Old Glory," as our national flag is sometimes called. The American Flag Association has laid down rules for its proper display, and the priest in charge of a church would be well advised to abide by them or inevitably there will be irate parishioners, protests to the rector and vestry, and possibly critical letters to the editor of the local newspaper. One could put up with such annoyances if a principle were involved, but in fact it isn't. Therefore, the easiest path is the one of least resistance.

The rule is that the American flag when displayed indoors should always be to the right of any other flag, or, if there are three flags, our national flag should be in the middle. In other words, it should always have the place of honor.

If the national flag is displayed in the nave, for example, it should be on the right side of the congregation, i.e., on the epistle side of the church. If, however, it is placed in the chancel, which to the American Flag Association is the same as a platform or dais, then it should be placed on the gospel side, for the rule is that it should be on the right side of a speaker's platform. Since a chancel is taken to be the equivalent of a stage, Old Glory belongs on the right of the altar. If an Episcopal church flag is also displayed, it should be placed on the opposite side from the American flag, that is, on the Gospel side if in the nave and on the epistle side if in the chancel.

This allows the parish priest an unexpected amount of latitude without infringing the rules. If, for example, he or she wished to have the church flag near the pulpit, but the pulpit was on the gospel side of the church, the two flags could be placed in the nave rather than in the chancel, thus reversing their proper places. If the pulpit is on the epistle side, the two flags could be located in the chancel instead of the nave. In both instances it would be quite proper to place the church flag on the same side as the pulpit.

Before the tumultuous sixties, the agony of the Vietnam War, and the humiliation of Watergate, Americans were generally patriotic and proud of their national colors. In consequence, it was not uncommon to have the Stars and Stripes carried in procession at the principal Sunday service in church. The costly war, however, and the disgraceful Nixon episode shattered many people's confidence in the wisdom and integrity of our governmental officials. American patriotism suffered a grievous blow, which among other things may have contributed to the decline of the custom of carrying the flag in procession, except on national holidays such as Independence Day.

FONTS

Being one of the two great sacraments of the gospel, (*Book of Common Prayer,* p. 858) baptism ranks with the eucharist in importance. Hence the font deserves an architectural setting of equal dignity to that of the altar. But such has not always been the case in the long and involved history of the church.

In the patristic period when it was the custom for those being baptized, adults as well as children, to remove all their old clothing, representing their former pagan life and priorities, and to be clothed after baptism in clean, white garments, representing their new life in Christ, it was thought unseemly to minister baptism in full view of the congregation. Instead, separate baptistries were built where the part of the initiatory sacrament that involved nudity could be ministered in private. After that, the newly baptized Christians were ushered into the church to join the faithful in the eucharist. The people did not witness the actual baptism, and, therefore, the font did not occupy a visual place of honor comparable to the altar.

The Easter Vigil, now happily recovered in the 1979 Prayer Book, was the accustomed time for baptism. Indeed, the season of Lent originated as a period of instruction for adult converts to Christianity, and it culminated in the great vigil when these catechumens were fully initiated into the church. An alternate time for baptism was the eve of Pentecost, perhaps because of the liturgical theme of the great feast. In baptism we receive the gift of the Spirit, thereby participating in the descent of the Holy Spirit upon the Church on Pentecost. The 1979 Prayer Book also appoints other days as especially appropriate for baptism: All

Saints' Day (or the Sunday after it), the Feast of the Baptism of our Lord (the first Sunday after the Epiphany), and any occasion when the bishop is present.

Although baptism played a conspicuous role in the expansion of the church after the time of Constantine, and we have the thrilling accounts of St. Remigius baptizing King Clovis together with three thousand of his Frankish subjects in A.D. 496, baptism declined in liturgical importance, when compared with the eucharist, after Europe had been largely converted and there was virtually no one left to baptize except newborn infants. The never-ending supply of babies would have provided enough candidates to make every Easter Vigil and Pentecost Eve an impressive liturgical spectacle had it not been for the exaggerated medieval concern with sin and damnation and the concomitant fear that infants who died unbaptized would be consigned to limbo, the cheerless abode of souls excluded from the full blessedness of the beatific vision. That bugaboo, plus high infant mortality, led to the practice of not waiting until Easter or Pentecost, but baptizing infants within a week of their birth and sooner if a child was puny and appeared to be in danger of death. It was often necessary, therefore, to administer baptism privately. And since there were relatively few to be baptized at the great feasts, the liturgical and architectural setting for baptism was far less impressive than that for the eucharist.

The 1549 Prayer Book contained two baptismal rites, one for public baptism of infants in church and the other for private baptism in houses. The 1662 Prayer Book added a third for "such as are of riper years." This was considered necessary because so many people had not been baptized during the Commonwealth period when the Prayer Book and its teachings had been suppressed and when the Anabaptists, who rejected infant baptism, were free to spread their doctrines. By 1660 there were many unbaptized adults in England for the first time in nearly a thousand years. This service was intended for them and also, to some degree, for the American colonies where there were pagans—Indians and blacks—as well as adult whites who had grown to maturity without having a church connection. The compilers of the 1662 Prayer Book expressed the hope that this service might prove useful "for the baptizing of Natives in our plantations, and others converted to the Faith."

Archbishop Cranmer in 1549 and the compilers of the 1662 Prayer Book considered private baptism to be a corrupt medieval practice, and they sought to restore the public administration of the sacrament. The 1662 Prayer Book did so by means of a rubric ordering baptisms to take place when congregations were present, that is, on Sundays and holy days. But as every sociologist knows, it is hard to change the ways of a nation quickly. The practice of private baptism continued and by the first half of the nineteenth century had become almost the rule. In this instance, the Ritualists and Ecclesiologists of the second half of the century, with their enthusiasm for medieval ways, did little to change the picture. It remained for the twentieth-century Liturgical Movement to make headway against the received tradition. In the last fifty years this movement has done much to change the liturgical habits of the Church and to bring them into conformity with biblical theology, early Christian practice, and the official formularies of the Anglican church.

By stressing the corporate nature of baptism and the importance of having those who are being added to the Church received, not by a mere handful of friends and relatives, but by a great congregation, the Liturgical Movement has accomplished what the sixteenth-century reformers set out to do but failed to achieve. And the 1979 Prayer Book gives full expression to the insights of the movement.

Early Christian fonts were of a variety of shapes: quadrilateral, hexagonal, and even cruciform. Round and oval ones came next and finally (in the sixth century) fonts shaped like a quatrefoil. Each shape was interpreted to convey some aspect of the meaning of baptism. The quadrilateral was said to suggest a coffin or a sarcophagus, since the believer is buried in baptism with Christ. The hexagonal and octagonal referred to the death of our Lord on the sixth day (Good Friday) of Holy Week and to his resurrection on the eighth day (the first day of the next week). Round and oval fonts were likened to the womb of the Virgin Mary. As our Lord "despised not the Virgin's womb" but was born into the world by means of it, so we are born again into the family of God by means of the font. As the saying goes, we who have God for our father (i.e., all baptized persons), have the Church for our mother. The font was perceived to be the womb of the Church.

Although rather plain except for their shape, early fonts were often surrounded by mosaics on domes, walls, and pavements, thus giving baptism the architectural setting it deserved, at least in the baptistries built to house the ministration of the sacrament. Later, the fonts themselves were decorated with carvings of appropriate symbols such as the ark (stressing salvation through baptism), fish (based on the *ichthus* symbol of Christ), and a cross (showing that by baptism we share in the victorious death of our Lord).

Early fonts were low, so that the candidate for baptism could stand in them. But the great majority of those that have survived are too shallow for submersion. Water was poured on the candidate's head. Known as "affusion," this method is permitted by the Prayer Book, as is "immersion," or dipping the candidate's head in the water. But "aspersion," or sprinkling a few drops of water on the person being baptized, is not allowed in Anglican formularies. Later in the Middle Ages when many infants but few adults were baptized, submersion came into use in the West as it had long been in the East, and fonts were raised on shafts or columns in order to make it easy for the priest to handle infants.

In the course of time, however, submersion went out of fashion in Europe but, of course, remained in use in the Orthodox church. By the fourteenth century, France generally used affusion. By the fifteenth century, Italy did so as well. In England, however, the change was not made until the Reformation.

As consecrated water was often left in the font for periods of time in the Middle Ages, font covers came into use to prevent the water from being taken surreptitiously for purposes of magic and witchcraft. Early medieval covers were flat, but by the fifteenth century they were often quite tall and elaborate, being ornamented with Gothic tracery, symbols, and polychrome. One English example, that of Thirsk, is no less than twenty-one feet tall. By contrast, most fonts made after the Reformation were relatively plain and uninteresting, although some of them were representatives of the passing styles of the Renaissance and the baroque periods.

By the late seventeenth and during the eighteenth centuries, the most common shape was that of a small vase or urn upon a slender pillar. Cherub head and acanthus leaves were among the favored decorations as, for example, the stone font in Christ Church, Lancaster County, Virginia, which dates to 1732. Symbols that were common on medieval fonts rarely appear on seventeenth-and eighteenth-century examples. With the Gothic Revival, however, fonts in medieval style reappeared and often displaced older models, which in some cases were passed along to small country missions or converted into garden ornaments or sundials. In more recent times, a great variety of shapes and materials have made their appearance including lucite fonts complete with falling water.

The eighty-first of the canons of 1604 ordered "that there shall be a font of stone in every church and chapel where baptism is to be ministered: the same to be set up in the ancient usual places," i.e., near the west door. In the words of one of the Caroline divines, Bishop Montague, this location was "to signify our entrance into God's church by baptism." It was required to be of stone, presumably, to prevent it from being moved elsewhere in the church for baptisms. Protestant dissenters generally preferred to place it near the pulpit when needed or else to use a silver bowl placed on the communion table for baptism. Puritan nonconformists in England periodically urged the bishops to allow fonts to be placed at the front of the church, close to the altar, so that the congregation might hear the rite and see the ceremony more easily.

A sermon preached in Durham Cathedral in 1628 recommended this on the grounds that the font and altar were "of equal worthiness," and therefore it made no sense to put one "at the head" and "the other at the foot" of the church. The speaker added, "Why are they not set in the body of the church or choir [i.e., the chancel], being the fittest place to receive the greatest assemblies?" Bishop Cosin, however, was unimpressed and refused to bring the font forward. In Cromwell's day, stone fonts were esteemed "popish," and silver bowls were used, instead, for baptisms.*

After the Restoration of Charles II, things which had been cast down were once more set up. When a group of Presbyterian divines at the Savoy Conference of 1661 requested that fonts be placed where the congregation could best see and hear, the bishops told them that "the font usually stands, as it did in primitive times, at or near the church door, to signify that baptism was the entrance into the church"** and dismissed the request with "the people may hear well enough" when the font is in its ancient location. Symbolism seems to have weighed more heavily with them than the auditory principle! But by way of leaning over backwards in order to be comprehensive, the bishops expressed their willingness to deal with hard cases by allowing the font to be moved to a more convenient place, but only with the express permission of the ordinary.

---

*J. G. Davies, *The Architectural Setting of Baptism,* London: Barrie & Rockliff, 1962, 98.
**Ibid., 100.

Many colonial churches observed Canon 81 and dutifully located the font near the door. Others, however, because of crowded naves and lack of space, moved their fonts to the front of the church, thereby weakening the Anglican tradition of having three separate liturgical centers: the font, pulpit, and altar. With the rise of the Evangelicals, the old tradition was swept away, and the three were placed together at the front, as was the case in Congregational, Presbyterian, and Baptist churches.

But the pendulum soon swung back again. The Catholic Revival, with its fondness for medieval ways, restored the received tradition, reconstituted the two-room church with its three distinct liturgical centers, and replaced the font—once more required to be of stone—at or near the west door. But in less than a century and a half, the Liturgical Movement, with its emphasis on the corporate nature of baptism and its insistence that it be ministered at the principal service on great feasts, has again created a desire to place the font near the front where large numbers of people can both hear the rite and see the ceremony.

Under the rubrics of the 1979 Prayer Book, it will no longer suffice to have a font stashed away in a chapel or baptistry that is out of the range of vision and hearing of the people in the nave. The font moreover must be placed so that the celebrant may "face the people across the font" (which means that it must be free-standing, not up against a wall) and so that the sponsors may "be so grouped that the people may have a clear view of the action" (which means that fonts can no longer be crowded into restricted space). This calls for a change in many existing locations. Changing liturgical practice requires a change in the setting of worship. All parish priests, vestries, and church architects please take notice.

Here is what Dr. Hatchett has to say by way of a guideline:

> The font should be in a prominent place, so that baptisms are visible, and so that it may serve as a constant reminder of baptism. It might be at the back of the nave near a principal door, in the chancel, on the floor of the nave, or at the center of a large entrance hall.
>
> Since the Book of Common Prayer gives precedence to immersion as the mode of baptism, the font might well be large enough for immersion: at the very least, it should be of significant size. The font, or the area around it, might be decorated with biblical types or symbols of baptism. A convenient table or shelf should be provided for books, towels, baptismal candles, and the chrism. An

aumbry (a locked case) for the chrism might be located near the font, and the Paschal candle should normally stand at the font, except during the Great Fifty Days. . . .

INCENSE*

From early times people found that certain gums and resins when burnt gave off a pleasing aroma, and they used "incense" (a word meaning "that which is burnt") in two distinct ways: (1) to sweeten the air and (2) to show honor to dignitaries. It was used in both these ways by the ancient Egyptians, Assyrians, Babylonians, and Persians, as well as by the Greeks, Romans, and Jews. Its fumigatory properties led to incense being used in connection with animal sacrifices, and for that reason it came to be associated with worship in the ancient world. The Mosaic law (Exodus 30:1-10) required its use every morning and evening at the altar of incense. And because it was costly, it was suitable as a gift for a king or as an offering to God and was regularly used in the temple at Jerusalem.

That the early Christians accepted incense is clear in the New Testament. The archangel Gabriel visited Zechariah while the latter was burning incense in the temple; also, the Magi brought incense along with gold and myrrh to the one who was born to be king. Moreover, in the vision of God and the Lamb in Revelation (5:8 and 8:3-5) the angel with a golden censer is said to have mingled incense with the prayers of all the saints, and the incense is identified as being or symbolizing prayer.

Because of the threat of persecution, however, early Christians often had to worship in secret and so could not use incense, which would be a dead giveaway. Besides, the developing claim from Domitian onwards that the emperors were to be the focus of the divinity of Rome resulted in the requirement that all citizens offer incense to his statue, which Christians could not in good conscience do and were often martyred for refusing to do. After the Peace of the Church in the fourth century, however, the liturgical use of incense made its appearance in Christian worship. Used at first for fumigatory purposes, chiefly at the burial of the dead, it soon came to be used also at the translation of relics of the saints and at the consecration of altars containing such relics. A separate honorific use also developed originating in the Roman civic

*Reprinted from *The Anglican* (Winter 1977).

ceremonial of carrying incense in procession before consuls and magistrates. After Constantine established Christianity as the state religion, bishops and priests were accorded the same public honors. Hence, the custom of censing the way of a bishop or his local representative, the priest, in procession to the altar is an inheritance from the fourth-century Roman Empire. The seventeenth-century *Ordo romanus Primus* prescribes this honorific use at the introit and at the gospel, both of them involving processions.

Centuries later, other regional uses, notably the Gallican, developed a more elaborate use with censing of the altar, the oblations, and the ministers, thus providing Percy Dearmer with a classic bad example. His *Parson's Handbook* practically opened with the dictum that "unintelligent accretion has always been the vice of religious ceremonial, details being added which came to be regarded as of sacred obligation as the generations pass, and in the end destroy the significance and beauty of the original rite." This happened, he declared, to the liturgical use of incense during the Middle Ages. By the fifteenth century the censings had become over-labored and even fussy, as had many other ceremonial actions in connection with the liturgy.

As a result of the Reformation, services were shortened and the ceremonial simplified. The Puritans in general disliked incense, but there was no universal objection to it. The near abolition of its liturgical use in England was merely a by-product of the reformer's attack on the sacrifice of the mass and the veneration of statues and relics. Because the Calvinists opposed the blessing of material objects, injunctions were issue in Edward VI's reign against censing images and bells but not against the use of incense as such. Nonetheless, its use declined sharply after 1549, except during Queen Mary's brief reign, but it did not disappear altogether, as churchwarden accounts and inventories of church ornaments clearly show. The continued use of incense was sporadic and of a modified character, so as not to bring down upon the parish priest the wrath of higher authorities. In most cases its use was confined to fumigating the church and sweetening the air before services. It was also used as an honorific on such occasions as the coronation of a king. Some liturgical use of incense persisted, for which we have documentary evidence. Lancelot Andrewes (1555-1626), the bishop of Winchester, and John Cosin (1594-1672), the bishop of Durham, are among the Caroline divines who regularly used it in worship. During Cromwell's ascendancy, its use was virtually nil, but its use was resumed after the Restoration of Charles II. By 1685, Archbishop Sancroft found sufficient need to compose and authorize a prayer for the blessing of a thurible. And we know that incense was burnt in procession at every royal coronation from Charles II to George III.

The Age of Reason, however, with its tinge of deism witnessed the decline and virtual extinction of the liturgical use of incense in England, largely because in the minds of rationalists incense was associated with medieval superstition. The last recorded public instance of its use was at Ely Cathedral in 1770 when a neurotic canon terminated a continuous tradition under pretense that it gave him a headache. The Evangelical Movement that followed did nothing to encourage its revival. The Evangelicals generally disliked medieval ways and considered them to be examples of superstition and popery. But the Oxford Movement prepared the way for its recovery, aided no doubt by Sir Walter Scott's novels and the Romantic Movement, which were nostalgic about the Middle Ages and popularized an overly favorable view of medieval life, thus helping to usher in the Gothic Revival. Details of the reintroduction of incense into Anglican worship form an unedifying part of our history. Other branches of the Church Catholic have fought and bled over great theological issues, but Anglicans have too often waxed hottest over trivial matters of ceremonial such as incense and articles of ecclesiastical attire.

Percy Dearmer was an advocate of the liturgical use of incense, as were the members of the Society of SS. Peter and Paul. The difference was that the latter wished to take over the elaborate contemporary Roman Catholic use of it, whereas the former held out for a scriptural and primitive ecclesiastical use, as an honorific before bishops and priests in procession, and as an offering to God at the Magnificat, the reading of the gospel, and at the offertory. This sample, ancient, and restrained use, he argued, would be the most beautiful and dignified in Christendom.

Subsequent modification in Roman practice and the return of a simpler Christian ceremonial have played into the hands of the Dearmerites. The use they favor goes well with the 1979 Prayer Book and with modern church architecture. Fussiness and jerking motions are out of favor, and there is no longer any need to cense persons or objects. All this belongs to a bygone period in church history when, in the view of many liturgical experts, corruption of primitive ways was rampant. In the words of Percy Dearmer, "The evil of all religious customs throughout history has been the piling up of trivial details: and both wisdom and learning are constantly needed to prevent the perpetuation of individual follies."

MEMORIALS, TOMBSTONES, and BOOKS OF REMEMBRANCE

Many persons gave or bequeathed land and money to parish churches in the course of the Middle Ages, which resulted in the creation of the office of churchwarden. The original function of these lay officials, later taken over by the vestry, was to serve as stewards or guardians of parochial endowments. Because of the marked concern of the medieval mind for sin and damnation, many such gifts were to build and endow chantry chapels and provide a stipend for priests to say daily masses in perpetuity for the souls of the donors in order to shorten their time in purgatory. As these chantry altars often occupied conspicious places in the church and were enclosed by parclose screens and provided with one or more seats for members of the family of the deceased, they restricted church interiors and tended to clutter them.

The chantry system, however, came to an abrupt end in the reign of Edward VI because of the vigorous opposition of the reformers to prayer for the dead and to noncommunicating masses. Moreover, the boy king's two Lord Protectors, the dukes of Somerset and Northumberland, rapaciously destroyed chantries and confiscated their endowments. After things settled down under Elizabeth I, the process of refurnishing the interiors of churches began, and the erection of memorials to the departed proceeded apace. Visitors to medieval English churches usually find many handsome memorials, often carved, sometimes polychromed, some of considerable artistic quality that date from her reign or from that of the Stuart kings.

Medieval memorials usually bore short inscriptions giving the names and dates of the deceased and a brief prayer for their souls. By the time of Elizabeth I, however, they began to grow wordier, often giving information about the forebears and relations of the deceased. Indeed, in some of them it is possible to read a family's history, for by that time connections by blood and marriage had become more important than ever before in determining one's position in society. Hence, those who composed the epitaphs rejoiced to record the dignities, attainments, and qualities of their departed relatives, partly to impress others and partly, perhaps, as a means of laying claim to a well-earned place in heaven for the deceased. In any event, Elizabethan and Jacobean memorial inscriptions are a far cry from the dread that accompanied death in the Middle Ages when an appeal for prayers for the soul of the deceased tended to eclipse his or her pride of place in terrestrial society.

By the second half of the seventeenth century, tombstones were used more and more in the American colonies, and by the eighteenth century memorial tablets were in evidence on church walls. An example of the former is the 1693 stone of Nathanial Bacon, the uncle of the Virginia rebel of the same name. (The stone is now in the tower entrance of Bruton Parish Church in Williamsburg.) In typical English style it declares, "Here lyeth ye body of Nathaniel Bacon, Esq., whose descent was from the Ancient House of the BACONS (one of which was Chancellor BACON and Lord Verulam) who was Auditor of Virginia and President of ye Honourable Councell of State and Commander in Chief of the County of York having been of the Councell for above 40 years and having always discharged ye offices in which he served with great Fidelity and Loyalty to his Prince. . . ." It is to the credit of those concerned that the stone records the interment, not of Colonel Bacon, but merely of his body, i.e., his mortal remains, a theological distinction generally observed in times past but not always in contemporary gravestone inscriptions. The rest of Bacon's inscription, however, although fascinating to antiquarians, looks suspiciously like a letter of recommendation to St. Peter to open wide the pearly gates and roll out the red carpet for the eminent and virtuous Virginia bigwig!

Eighteenth century memorial inscriptions were even more grandiloquent and, toward the end of the century, sometimes as sentimental as their Victorian successors. One amusing example is the wall tablet in Bruton Parish Church erected to the memory of Dr. William Cocke (1672–1720) by his son in 1752. It lists the good doctor's achievements and virtues and records that he "died suddenly, sitting a Judge upon the Bench of the General Court in the Capitol" in 1720 and that his friend Governor Spotswood "attended his Funeral and weeping, saw the Corps Interred at the West Side of the Altar in this Church." In most respects, the inscription was characteristic of the time, but in one respect it was exceptional. His son was averse to the custom of making such of the ancestry of the deceased. He observed in a letter to his sister that he did not wish to add their father to the numerous company of "just men made perfect by their epitaphs." He was content to state his father's origin in these laconic words: "An English Physician, Born of reputable Parents. . . ."

Like their counterparts in the mother country, many old churches in America accumulated numerous memorials by the end of the nineteenth century, so that in some cases they gave the interiors a somewhat cluttered appearance and tended to distract the attention of worshipers from the chief liturgical centers and from the eucharistic action. With the rise of the Liturgical Movement in recent decades, with its reemphasis upon those centers and upon the action, a resistance to such memorials has discouraged the addition of new ones—especially large and wordy ones. Indeed, in some churches the elaborate wall tablets of yesteryear have been removed from the chancel and nave, and have been relocated in less conspicuous places, such as the narthex or parish house.

There is no overpowering reason why we should not continue to introduce memorial tablets into our churches, but, all things considered, it would be well to keep them small and inconspicuous so as not to detract from the liturgical action. Also, care should be taken in the case of tombstones to insure the theological accuracy of the inscriptions, especially in the opening phrase "Here lies the body of" or "the mortal remains of" the deceased.

Care should also be taken in composing inscriptions. They should be brief and devoid of Pelagian overtones. And an improper juxtaposition of phrases must be guarded against. St. George's Church in Lee, Massachusetts, has a wall tablet in memory of its founder and first senior warden. After exalting his faith in God and his diligent service to the parish, the tablet states that the worthy gentlemen died suddenly on a particular Sunday after "having attended both Morning and Evening Prayer in the Church." The statement is undoubtedly true. But as it comes across to the reader, it is hardly an encouragement to worship twice on one Sunday in St. George's Church!

A modern alternative to memorial tablets is the use of a Book of Remembrance, which has made its appearance in many churches. It should be of the highest quality rag paper, handsomely bound, and with the names of the deceased neatly lettered. And it should be enclosed in a well-lighted, glass-topped stand, and a plan established to turn a page every day, or every week, so that each name receives exposure at regular intervals. Care ought to be taken to locate it in the church or narthex where it is readily seen yet unlikely to impede processions or the comings and goings of worshipers.

ORGANS and CHOIRS

Early Christians were aware of the Jewish practice of having a choir take part in the temple services, because they are referred to in the Old Testament. As soon as the Church emerged from the shadows and became the official religion of the Roman Empire, the use of choirs became widespread. The fact that the psalms were sung antiphonally by Christians in the fourth century is considered evidence of a conscious link between Jewish tradition and evolving church practice.

Wind instruments are very ancient and appear in all pastoral societies. They are mentioned often in the Old Testament, e.g., Gen. 4:21; 1 Sam. 10:5; 1 Kings 1:40; Job 21:12 and 30:31; and Psalm 150:4. Eventually the organ appeared among the Greeks at least as early as the third century B.C. Among early known examples in England were those of Malmesbury (eighth century) and Glastonbury and Winchester (tenth century). By the thirteenth century they had become common in cathedrals, abbeys, and larger parish churches. By the end of the Middle Ages the organ was almost universal.

Luther, being musical, valued the organ as an accompaniment of his chorales, but Calvin objected to church organs because they were not specifically authorized in the New Testament and because he feared the possible abuse of music's emotional power. English Calvinists tried several times to persuade Queen Elizabeth I and the bishops to order them removed from all churches, but the authorities would not accede to their wishes. Biding their time until their numbers and power waxed, the Puritans eventually rebelled against Charles I, and when they succeeded in dominating parliament an act was passed in 1644 mandating the destruction of all church organs. So effectively was it carried out under Cromwell that very few pre-Commonwealth organs survived, and those few were saved by being removed to private homes.

After the Restoration of crown and church in 1660, organs once more made their appearance in Anglican churches. By the eighteenth century some cathedrals, Chapels Royal, and larger parish churches had rather fine ones, but many of the smaller and rural parish churches were content with barrel organs with a limited selection of tunes.

By the eighteenth century colonial churches began to acquire organs, although they were largely confined to the wealthier churches, especially those in towns. Early examples in Virginia are Petsworth Parish Church (1737), Hungars Church (c. 1751), Suffolk Church (1753), Bruton Parish Church (1755), and Stratton Major Parish Church (c. 1767). In churches that were not fortunate enough to have an organ, the clerk (or layreader) opened the tune for the metrical psalms and a few hymns by means of a tuning fork or a pitch pipe.

The sixteenth-century reformers deplored the corrupt state of liturgical practice in the Western church. With respect to music, they objected to the use of elaborate settings that only trained choirs could sing. Their objection rested on the grounds that the people in the nave were excluded from musical participation in the service and reduced to a passive audience. In an attempt to make the eucharist and other services more corporate, Archbishop Cranmer not only simplified the rite and translated it into English in 1549, he also engaged John Merbecke to compose simple settings for the new Prayer Book on the principle of one note to a syllable. This appeared in 1550. Some of his settings, which still bear his name, have been widely used since their revival in the nineteenth century.

The continental reformers had no wish to abolish choirs. Luther introduced the chorale in order to encourage congregational singing. But he also wished to preserve those devotional elements that only a trained choir could provide. Calvin, unlike Luther, objected to church organs, but he nonetheless favored retaining choirs in order to lead corporate singing. So it was that the Reformation gave church choirs a double role: in addition to their medieval function as performers of music beyond the capacity of the people, they were now to lead the congregation in psalmody and hymnody.

Except for the interruption of the Commonwealth in the years 1649–60, English cathedrals with their endowed choirs continued to carry on the choral services on a daily basis, thus perpetuating medieval tradition. By the end of the seventeenth century, Anglican chant developed out of the plainsong psalm-tones then in use, and it became widely popular throughout the Anglican Communion about the middle of the nineteenth century.

Parish churches in the eighteenth century, both in England and America, developed what has jocularly been called "cock and hen" choirs, composed of both men and women. Cathedral choristers, of course, wore surplices and occupied stalls in the chancel, but village choirs wore their street clothes and occupied the west gallery where the organ was usually located.

When the recent Princeton graduate Philip Fythian, became a tutor at the country seat of Councillor Robert Carter of Nomini Hall on the Northern Neck of Virginia in 1774, he attended Nomini Church on Sunday and "was surprised when the Psalm began, to hear a large collection of voices singing at the same time from a Gallery." He was a Presbyterian just getting acquainted with Anglican ways, hence the choir came as a surprise to him.*

The coming of the Ritualists and Ecclesiologists in the middle of the nineteenth century brought pressure to bear on parish churches to copy not only the architectural setting of worship but also the choral services of cathedrals. Therefore, organs and choirs in thousands of parish churches were removed from west galleries and relocated in chancels especially deepened to accommodate them, often provided with a rood screen, thus imitating the interior arrangement of cathedrals. By the end of the nineteenth century, all but a few parish churches were thus transformed.

As chancels cannot contain large organs, they were usually placed on either or both sides of the chancel behind walls that were pierced in order to allow the sound to come through. This proved disastrous from a musical point of view because much of the volume and tone were lost. Making organs larger and more powerful helped cure the former, but never completely overcame the latter. Although it fitted the liturgical practice of the day, it remained a problem from a musical point of view.

The Liturgical Movement, however, with its emphasis on the corporate nature of the eucharist, elicited serious complaints about deep chancels and about placing the choir between the altar and the people. At the early eucharist in particular, when there was no choir, the celebrant was separated from the congregation by an expanse of empty choir stalls, and there arose a desire to bring priest and people closer together. This was accomplished either by setting up a nave altar or by relocating the organ and choir at the rear of the nave, often in the west gallery.

This change is taking place all over the country and, once the people have grown accustomed to it, the change has generally proved successful. It reduces the clutter of furnishings in the chancel, opens more space for a freestanding altar, and provides adequate seating capacity for the variety of ministers that modern

---

*Hunter D. Farish, ed., *Journal and Letters of Philip Vickers Fythian* 1773-1774 Williamsburg, VA: Colonial Williamsburg, 1943.

liturgical practice has brought into being: crucifer, taperers, banner bearers, thurifers and chalicists. Relocating the organ in the rear gallery has also paid dividends in that it affords more efficient use of smaller organs and serves more effectively to bolster congregational singing, for it goes without saying that it is better for corporate worship to have the support of the organ and choir come from behind the people in the nave to bolster their singing, than to have it come from the front of the church as though it were a performance for an audience.

PAINTINGS, MURALS, and WALL RELIEFS (see also TABLETS OF THE LAW and STATIONS OF THE CROSS)

When Christianity became the established religion of the Roman Empire, large and handsome churches were built. Judging from the documents of the time and from surviving examples such as Santa Sophia in Constantinople and the churches in Ravenna and elsewhere, their interiors were often richly decorated with colorful mosaics and icons, for these two-dimensional works of art, rather than statuary and bas-relief, were the chief outlet for the artistic enthusiasm of the Orthodox church.

Indeed, Santa Sophia, built in the sixth century, with its gigantic dome and vast interior, was the greatest church in Christendom, and it must have been breathtaking to enter it in its heyday when its interior was ablaze with color. Even five centuries later the power of its magnificence was strong enough to be a factor in winning the Russians to the Orthodox church, rather than to the Latin church of the West.

The eleventh-century duke of Kiev, Vladimir, having decided to become a Christian, could not decide between the Latin and Greek forms of Christianity. According to legend, he sent ambassadors to both Rome and Constantinople to see for themselves. The report from Rome, which was only beginning to emerge from the Dark Ages, was far from enthusiastic, for St. Peter's before the time of Brumante was not very impressive. But the other report was euphoric. "When we stood in the temple [i.e., Santa Sophia]," the emissary declared, "we did not know where we were, for there is nothing else like it on earth: there in truth God has his dwelling with men, and we can never forget the beauty we saw there."*

---

*Frank E. Wilson: *The Divine Commission* New York: Morehouse-Barlow Co., 1940, 112.

Beauty and holiness are so closely linked that Valdimir and his people were convinced and accepted baptism at the hands of Byzantine priests. And Holy Russia, thereafter, was a bastion of Orthodox Christianity—all because of the beauty of the interior of one church! A further note on Santa Sophia: although the venerable edifice still stands, its gorgeous interior was partially destroyed after the conquest of Constantinople by the iconoclastic Turks in 1453 who whitewashed the mosaics and converted the church into a mosque, complete with minarets. Partially restored in the nineteenth century, and more completely in the twentieth, the precious relic of early Christian architecture is now a museum.

The concept of beauty as akin to holiness also took root in the Western church and produced the great cathedrals and churches of the Middle Ages. The Western ethos, however, was partial to carving in both wood and stone, and expressed its love of color in polychroming and stained-glass windows. Although surviving medieval churches have much of their carved statuary and tracery and some of their stained-glass windows, few of them have retained the rich polychroming that by the fifteenth century made their interiors almost as colorful as Santa Sophia itself. Illuminated manuscripts, however, have survived in quantity and often depict church interiors as they were seen by medieval worshipers. Churches of that day were like museums and treasure houses. By contrast with the thatched cottages with mud floors and the drab lives of the peasants, the churches must have been exciting and uplifting places to visit if for no other reason than their beauty, color, and richness.

Just as the Muslims in their austere religious zeal covered over the mosaics of Santa Sophia, so that extreme Protestants whitewashed the interior of many a Gothic church, obliterating the "dooms" on chancel arches and otherwise destroying or removing all manner of medieval works of art. Reformers of the Calvinistic type, such as Martin Bucer and Peter Martyr, who came to England in Edward VI's reign, were so much in favor of intellectualizing religion that they were openly opposed to outward symbols of devotion and feared the emotional appeal of religious art. The unscrupulous duke of Northumberland, as Lord Protector of the boy king, authorized the pillaging of churches. Enormous harm was done in the years he was in power, 1549–53. If he had remained any longer, much that has come down to us would have been lost as well.

This whirlwind of vandalism and destruction changed under the queens Mary and Elizabeth, and the refurnishing and embellishment of churches began. They were greatly beautified during the golden age of Elizabeth, when England enjoyed a period of prosperity. The work continued under James I and Charles I. But the success of the parliamentary army under Cromwell initiated the second era of vandalism and destruction during which the churches of England were stripped of many organs, stained-glass windows, gold and silver communion plate, and other works of art —all because of the well-meaning but misguided zeal of the Puritans.

After the Restoration of Charles II and during the Georgian period, handsome churches were built by architects such as Sir Christopher Wren (1632-1723) and James Gibbs (1682-1754). Old churches as well as new ones were embellished by the exquisite work of woodcarvers such as Grinling Gibbons (1648-1721). Although English churches of the seventeenth and eighteenth centuries were somewhat more restrained in their interior decoration than the more flamboyant baroque churches on the continent, they were sufficiently ornate to be quite distinct from Protestant churches generally, especially the meetinghouses of the Congregationalists, Presbyterians, Baptists, and Quakers.

Although Anglican churches in the colonies were, on the whole, plainer than their English counterparts, those in the larger towns were sometimes as well designed and as handsomely decorated as their contemporaries in the mother country: King's Chapel and Christ Church, Boston; St. Paul's Chapel, New York; Christ Church and St. Peter's, Philadelphia; and St. Michael's, Charleston.

King's Chapel, built 1749-54, had an altarpiece with gilded cherub heads, a dove, and an IHS in a glory. Later, Benjamin West painted a "Last Supper" for its altarpiece. The rural Maryland Church, St. Barnabas (Prince George's County), had a "Last Supper" behind the altar as early as 1722, attributed to Gustavus Hesselius (1682-1755), the portrait painter from Sweden. Another country church—St. Andrew's near Leonardtown, Maryland— paid 16 10s. currency in 1771 to John Friech, a "limner," to paint an altarpiece containing the Decalogue, creed, paternoster, and some selections from Exodus. The vestry provided "Lamp Black, white Vitriol and a Book of Gold Leaf." Another bit of color was introduced into St. Michael's, Charleston, built 1752-61, when the ceiling over the altar, following English practice, was painted blue with gold stars—no doubt to point up the cosmic significance of the sacrament of the altar!

These baroque refinements, needless to say, did not appeal to the Evangelicals, who generally found the lettering of key texts from the Bible more congenial. But the Ecclesiologists who ushered in the Gothic Revival loved statuary, polychroming, tracery, stenciling, and encaustic tiles—all of which enriched their church interiors and made them different from those of the Evangelicals.

Color and elaborate interior decoration were by no means confined to neo-Gothic churches. The interior of H. H. Richardson's magnificent Trinity Church, Boston, built 1872-77 in Romanesque style, is completely covered with mural decoration done under the supervision of John LaFarge, who also designed the superb stained-glass windows that fill the west front. Other windows are by William Morris and Sir Edward Burne-Jones. In Roger Kennedy's words, Trinity Church represents "the full panoply of Victorian grandeur."*

Just as, in James Russell Lowell's words, "new occasions teach new duties, time makes ancient good uncouth," so the rise of contemporary art and architecture in the twentieth century has affected taste and left its mark on churches. The changed concepts are, perhaps, nowhere more graphically manifest than in the new Coventry Cathedral, which is a touchstone for contemporary ecclesiastical style, and more and more spinoffs of it appear in this country as year succeeds to year. Although avant garde in style, Conventry Cathedral is traditional with respect to the interior arrangement for worship. Indeed, it ignores in so many ways the principles of the Liturgical Movement that it has been called "the last of the Cambridge Movement cathedrals."

PEWS and SEDILIA

Contrary to what most people suppose, seating in the naves of churches was virtually unknown for the first thousand years or more of Christian history. People normally stood during the eucharist. This was the customary posture of worshipers. It is to this day in Eastern churches. No seats were provided for the congregation at large, but, as a concession to the elderly and infirm, stone seats were eventually attached to the walls or to the piers of the nave, which gave rise to the phrase "pushed to the wall," for those who were unequal to the physical fatigue of standing for long periods of time.

---

*Roger G. Kennedy, *American Churches* (New York: Crossroad, 1982), 275.

By about the thirteenth century, benches were gradually introduced into English parish churches. By the end of the Middle Ages, they were not only common but substantial, with backs and ends often elaborately carved with figures of saints, symbols of our Lord's Passion, and fanciful animals. The late medieval period, after the Black Death had reduced the number of serfs and raised the pay of free laborers, witnessed the high watermark of the woodcarvers' skills. Existing pews of that period bear witness to their achievements. These pews were arranged in islands or blocks and did not come right up to the chancel or to the west wall so as to leave room for processions.

After the Reformation, nave pews tended to increase in both size and number, and naves became crowded with pews high enough to make foot warmers effective but which screened the occupants from their neighbors. Although practical in unheated churches, these box pews militated against Archbishop Cranmer's desire to make the liturgy visually more corporate.

Parish church interiors by the eighteenth century were often cluttered further by the practice of the landed gentry building large box pews at their own expense and furnishing them with cushioned seats, carpets, and other comforts that set them off from their less fortunate fellow parishioners. Box pews with high sides also help to explain why pulpits had to be elevated, and why "wineglass" pulpits were so common in colonial days. In order to be seen by worshipers ensconced in such pews, the preacher had to be "high and lifted up," like Yahweh in Isaiah's vision in the Temple.

In the course of the nineteenth century most high pews were cut down or done away with because stoves were introduced into churches and the worshipers wished to benefit from radiation and convection, which the old high box pews impeded. In most cases they were replaced by slip pews or benches, too frequently of poor design and often with seats too narrow for comfort. The Gothic Revival did much to correct the situation, so that by the end of the nineteenth century most churches had pews of good design and materials.

In more recent times, beginning perhaps with the Cathedral of St. John the Divine and the Washington Cathedral, there has been a growing preference for well-made chairs rather than pews. They are less expensive, provide greater flexibility, and can easily be rearranged for such occasional events as a Christmas pageant or a morality play. Whatever is done, however, it is important to plan carefully the seating in a church both from the point of the comfort of the worshipers and in regard to the proportions of the building and the requirements of the liturgy.

Seats for the celebrant, the deacon, and the subdeacon came into use in England about the twelfth century—only a hundred years before seats in the nave. Called "sedilia" (Latin for seats), they were usually located on the south side of the chancel and were three in number. The priest and his two assistants occupied them during those parts of the eucharist when they were free to sit down, that is, when the choir sang the gloria, kyrie, and creed, as well as during the chanting of the psalms and the reading of the lessons other than the gospel. In England the sedilia were usually stone seats built into a niche in the wall. On the continent, however, wooden seats were more common, and in the late Middle Ages they were often richly carved and surmounted by arches or canopies.

During the Georgian period, the priest was usually provided with a box pew, known as the "rector's pew," near the crossing or near the pulpit. Matins, the litany, and antecommunion were read there, and there was no need to have a seat for him within the altar rails, for he would have no occasion to sit down from the offertory, when he went to the altar, until the end of the service. Moreover, in colonial days curates were rare, and crucifers, taperers, banner bearers, and chalicists had not yet made their appearance. Hence, there was no need for sedilia or for any other seating in the sanctuary.

All this was changed by the Victorian Ecclesiologists, who largely succeeded in reviving medieval practices. Thereafter, the celebrant went immediately to the altar at the beginning of the eucharist and needed a place to sit. Also, deacons and subdeacons were much in evidence. They, too, had to be accommodated. So, medieval-type sedilia were introduced into many churches of Gothic style and highbacked chairs of Chippendale design into those of Georgian style.

Modern practice has tended to reverse the change brought about by the Ecclesiologists in this respect. Now, as in colonial days, the priest is encouraged to make a ceremonial distinction between the Ministry of the Word and that of the sacrament by occupying a seat in the chancel until after the sermon and to approach the altar at the offertory. But the Liturgical Movement has initiated yet another change that is reflected in the rubrics of the 1979 Prayer Book. These have been summaried by Dr. Hatchett in these words:

A chair for the celebrant or officiant should be in a visible position. It should be easily moveable so that it can be placed at the entrance to the chancel for confirmations and ordinations. It is sometimes best for the celebrant's chair to be on a low platform, but it must not be raised so high that it looks like a throne. Chairs and benches for assisting ministers should be grouped about the chair of the chief celebrant. The chairs should have arms and shelves (or there should be a shelf or table nearby) for books needed in the course of the service.

All that needs to be added by way of explanation and warning is that the platform serves to elevate the celebrant sufficiently so that when seated his or her upper torso is visible to the congregation in the nave. Otherwise, the celebrant may appear to be a latter-day John the Baptist's head on a charger! Care must always be taken to prevent solemn occasions from appearing ridiculous.

PULPITS and LECTERNS

Since the preaching of the Word has been an invariable practice of the Church since the days of the Apostles, one might suppose that pulpits, like altars, have always been a part of a church's furnishings. The truth is, however, that the pulpit, in the sense of an elevated stand in the nave for a preacher, is a medieval innovation. In early Christian days, the bishop as the guardian of the faith preached from his "cathedra," i.e., the bishop's chair or throne, and its original position was behind the altar. A rare survival of this ancient placement of the bishop's cathedra can be seen in Norwich Cathedral. Later the "ambo," a raised platform from which lessons were read, came to be used for sermons as well. Still later, in the Middle Ages, the rood loft (atop the rood screen) was used for preaching. Finally, a separate structure, usually at the north side of the nave, came to be the normal location for preachers. Known as the "pulpit" from a Latin word meaning a scaffold or stage, it became general in parish churches by the end of the Middle Ages. Among famous pre-Reformation pulpits on the continent are the marble ones at Pisa and Siena. Late medieval English pulpits, usually of wood, were often richly carved. In addition, stone pulpits were sometimes placed against the outside walls of churches—as, for example, at Magdalene College, Oxford— for preaching to outdoor congregations.

With its renewed interest in Holy Scripture and its great emphasis on preaching, the Reformation made pulpits more important than ever before. Also the appearance of the English Prayer Book in 1549 resulted in a renewed emphasis on hearing what the priest said. Formerly, when the mass was in Latin, which few people in the nave understood, the celebrant was under no compulsion to raise his voice or to speak distinctly. After 1549, however, this changed abruptly, and a rearrangement of church interiors was undertaken in the interests of audibility. Instead of mumbling the mass in a low voice at the altar far removed from the people, the celebrant now read it in a loud voice, most of it from a reading desk connected to the pulpit in the nave where he could be heard. The priest and people did not go forward to the altar in the chancel until after the confession. Those intending to receive the sacrament, by going into the chancel, stood or knelt near the altar where they could hear the prayer of consecration and see the manual acts. This practice explains the phrase in the invitation to confession. The operative words were these: "Draw near with faith, and take this holy sacrament to your comfort. . . ." That was the signal to go forward into the chancel. Those who were "minded to receive the Holy Communion" did so, and the rest of the congregation left the church and went home.

Because of this new development, the pulpit (with its attached reading desk) took on a new dimension of significance. The towering structure stood in the popular mind for more than sermons alone. From the sixteenth to the nineteenth centuries it was as much a symbol of liturgical worship as it was of preaching, because people were accustomed to hearing Morning Prayer, the litany, and antecommunion read from it, as well as lessons and sermons. It was only from the offertory onwards that communicants forsook the nave for the chancel.

As has been pointed out, the attempt to make the rite more audible, and therefore more obviously corporate, resulted in the novel practice of combining the pulpit and reading desk (or lectern) into one structure, thereby producing the "two-decker," for the reading desk was at a lower level than the pulpit. As time went on, the clerk's desk was added, thus producing the "three-decker," which was so familiar in George Washington's day. From the lowest level of the structure, the clerk (or lay reader) read lessons and pitched the tune for the metrical psalms.

Because of its unwieldy size, the three-decker tended to obscure the view of the altar. When a church had side galleries, the massive structure could not be placed against the north or south wall of the nave. The resulting problem was sometimes solved by placing it at the head of the nave, directly in front of the altar, where it would obscure the view of the altar for the least number of worshipers yet positioning the priest where he could best be heard and seen by those in the galleries as well as those in the nave. Curiously enough, this location was not construed to be an upstaging of the altar by the pulpit, as we might suppose today. The prevailing medieval concept of the two-room church and the rigid distinction in worshipers' minds between the chancel and nave had survived. Trinity Church, Newport, Rhode Island, built in 1725, still has this interior arrangement—alone of all surviving colonial churches.

Churches built or retrofitted by Evangelicals and some High Church bishops such as Hobart and Dehon often had pulpits placed in the center of the east end behind rather than in front of the holy table. This arrangement gave little credence to the notion that chancels should be distinct from naves. Instead, all three of the liturgical centers were placed together, as in Presbyterian and Baptist churches, Evangelical pulpits were massive, like their medieval counterparts as modified by the Jacobeans and Georgians. Often placed where altars formerly stood, these pulpits visually dominated church interiors, as befitted those who placed such emphasis on the Word. An unpretentious table was placed in front of and below the pulpit for use at Holy Communion. Never before was the visible symbol of the Blessed Sacrament so effectively subordinated to that of the Word!

But this proved to be yet another passing phase. The Ecclesiologists soon made both the surviving Georgian three-deckers and the early nineteenth-century way of arranging church interiors the object of their articulate contempt. Within scarcely more than half a century, most churches of the Anglican communion responded to what the Ecclesiologists considered to be "proper" and rearranged their interiors along medieval lines with the pulpit and reading desk separated and relocated on opposite sides of the central aisle of the nave. Reading desks, moreover, were generally replaced by lecterns, often in the form beloved by the Caroline divines—that of a brass eagle.

The eventual rise of the Liturgical Movement, however, has tended to obliterate once more the medieval notion of the rigid distinction between chancel and nave. It has also encouraged the use of freestanding altars—and even centrally located ones. This loosening of the received tradition has slipped the cable, so to speak, that formerly anchored the pulpit to the nave. Now it is to be found in various locations as best fits the circumstances of each church. In those with centrally placed altars (and in other experimental churches), the pulpit, often much smaller than formerly, is sometimes located within the altar rails—a peculiarity of the early nineteenth century that was rigorously opposed by the Ecclesiologists.

Dr. Hatchett's observations concerning the implications of the 1979 Prayer Book with respect to pulpits follows:

> The pulpit symbolizes Christ's presence in his Word as the altar symbolizes his presence in the eucharistic sacrament. Ideally, one pulpit should be used for the lessons, the gradual psalm, the Gospel, and the sermon; and also for the Exsultet at the Easter Vigil. It should be a prominent piece of furniture that can accommodate a large Bible, and with a shelf for other books or items. Its construction and placement should allow torchbearers to stand near the reader. It should be accessible so that lectors, the cantor, the reader of the Gospel, the preacher and possibly the leader of the Prayers of the People can make their way to and from it easily and with dignity.

RESERVED SACRAMENT

As early as the second century there are references to the practice of reserving the eucharistic elements—usually the bread alone— for the benefit of those who could not be present at the weekly celebration. Such a practice is mentioned in Justin Martyr's *Apology* (c. 155) and frequently referred to by Tertullian (160-220), St. Cyprian (d. 258), and St. Basil (d. 379). Devout persons, especially hermits who lived far from a church, sometimes kept the Blessed Sacrament in their homes or on their persons, so that they might receive Holy Communion daily or at least more frequently than they could attend church. This custom survived, particularly among hermits, until the thirteenth or fourteenth century. Reservation also proved to be beneficial for those who were unable to be present at the Sunday eucharist because of travel, sickness, imprisonment, or the requirements of secular employment.

After the time of Constantine, churches became the usual places for reservation. The sacrament was kept either in the sacristy or in the church itself, and various ways of reserving it came into use. One way was in an "aumbry," a cupboard in a wall of the church or sacristy. Medieval aumbries were usually large enough to accommodate sacred vessels, relics, books, as well as the reserved sacrament. According to the Anglican liturgical scholar Dom

Gregory Dix, O.S.B., the use of aumbries for reservation was rare in medieval days. But thanks to the Ecclesiologists and Percy Dearmer they have become common throughout the Anglican Communion.

Aumbries were forbidden for this purpose in the Roman church in 1863 in the interest of encouraging the use of tabernacles. But the rule has been relaxed in recent years in certain instances. Rome no less than Canterbury has responded to the Liturgical Movement, and its insights have brought their ceremonial practices closer together than at any time since the Middle Ages.

A variant of the aumbry that was especially popular in late medieval Germany, Belgium, and France was the "sacrament house"—a tall, shrine-like receptable for the Reserved Sacrament. It developed from the stone niche in the wall (that held the aumbry) after the institution in 1264 of the Feast of Corpus Christi and eventually took the form of a small tower, the central part of which was done in openwork. They were often objects of beauty, decorated with carved reliefs representing the Last Supper, the Passion and related subjects. After the sixteenth century, however, they were increasingly replaced by "tabernacles" or boxes set in the middle of the altar to hold the reserved species. Tabernacles were virtually unknown in England until they were introduced by the Victorian Ritualists, many of whom mistakenly thought them medieval.

Another way of reserving the sacrament was in a hanging "pyx," a container suspended over or in front of the altar. Medieval examples are often of precious metal and sometimes wrought in the shape of a dove. According to Dr. Dearmer, the hanging pyx was "the more general method of reservation" in medieval England, hence the Ecclesiologists espoused it along with the aumbry.

The Dearmerites encouraged the use of hanging pyxes, but they had only partial success until the Liturgical Movement made freestanding altars popular. Since it is impracticable to have a tabernacle on such an altar, other means of reservation needed to be found. That, more than anything else, explains the disappearance of tabernacles and their widespread replacement by aumbries and hanging pyxes.

From early days in both the Eastern and Western church, reservation appears to have been confined to the bread. After the eleventh century, however, the Orthodox dipped the host into the consecrated wine and reserved it after it had dried. In this form it was used for the communion of the sick and for the liturgy of the presanctified in Lent.

Archbishop Cranmer's first *Book of Common Prayer* (1549) allowed the priest to reserve a portion of the Blessed Sacrament at an ordinary mass and carry it later to the sick, or, if preferred, the priest could celebrate a private eucharist in the sick person's home. The 1552 Prayer Book, however, did not specifically authorize reservation nor did Queen Elizabeth's 1559 Prayer Book, although, curiously enough, her Latin version of the *Book of Common Prayer* did!

The 1662 Prayer Book ordered whatever remained of the consecrated elements to be consumed immediately after the blessing, which would appear to forbid reservation. It has been argued by scholars, however, that this rubric was intended to prevent the sacred elements from being used for secular purposes. During the Cromwellian interlude, Puritan-minded clergy were said to be in the habit of taking what was left over in order to feed their numerous progeny! Even so, the rubric caused controversy and litigation when the Victorian Ritualists endeavored to revive the practice of reservation for the purpose of sick communions and were vigorously opposed by the stalwart Evangelicals.

After the dust settled, reservation for that purpose became increasingly common in both England and the United States. It is interesting that both the Dearmerites and the supporters of the Society of SS. Peter and Paul favored it. Also interesting is the fact that in the Scottish Episcopal church reservation remained customary in the eighteenth and nineteenth centuries, and the Scottish Prayer Book specifically authorizes it.

With its emphasis on the eucharist as the corporate act of the whole body of the faithful and not just of the priest, the Liturgical Movement has cast doubt upon the idea of private communions and has given new impetus to administering the Reserved Sacrament to the sick and others unable to attend church for the eucharist. This not only makes the service shorter (which is sometimes a great boon to the infirm) but also points up the fact that the sick person, although physically unable to be in church on Sunday or a holy day, is enabled to participate in the eucharist by means of receiving a portion of the sacred elements that were consecrated by the corporate act of priest and people on that occasion.

Marion Hatchett has this to say about the implications of the 1979 Prayer Book with respect to the place of reservation:

> Since the Prayer Book implies that Communion of those unable to attend a public celebration is normally to be from the reserved

Sacrament, and since it provides for Good Friday Communion from elements consecrated at the Maundy Thursday celebration, and allows administration by a deacon, a church building should have a place for the reservation of the eucharistic elements. An aumbry might be fixed in the wall of the sacristy or of a chapel, or on a side wall of the chancel, out of normal line of vision of the congregation. Preferably, the eucharistic sacrament is not reserved on or behind an altar at which the Eucharist is celebrated.

SIDE ALTARS and CHAPELS

The early Christians developed the principle of having one—and only one—altar in a church, and the people of God gathered around it for a celebration of the eucharist once each Lord's Day. In the course of time, however, the church became the official religion of the empire and eventually grew enormously in wealth and numbers. By the Middle Ages there were a great many priests, each of whom was expected to celebrate the eucharist frequently—even daily. Under this multiplication of masses the old principle broke down. Additional altars were needed, and they soon appeared, not only in great cathedrals and monastic chapels but also in parish churches in the form of side altars, chapel altars, and chantry altars.

Side altars placed against the walls of the nave or transept took little space and could be used not only for weekday masses but also as ambos or lecterns for the liturgy of the Word on Sundays. Today, of course, they may conveniently serve as stations for ministering Holy Communion on great feast days to large congregations.

In their attempt to recover primitive Christian practice and make the eucharist more corporate, the reformers rejected the idea of noncommunicating masses. In effect, this limited the eucharist in most churches to Sundays and holy days when there was a reasonable expectation of having a congregation, and it ruled out solitary celebrations. Hence, chantry chapels were dismantled and side altars removed. Except for cathedrals, where a few chapels (often used for daily offices) continued in use, churches generally had only one altar down to the nineteenth century when nostalgia for the Middle Ages impelled the Ecclesiologists to recover many things that had fallen into disuse.

The last century and a half witnessed the reappearance of side altars in parish churches, not so much to provide each priest with a separate altar for daily celebrations as for a convenient location for weekday eucharists where a small congregation could be near the celebrant, which would scarcely be the case if it took place at the high altar yet much less expensive than building a chapel.

The Liturgical Movement has put such stress on the freestanding high altar as the proper place for the people of God to gather around for the corporate action of the eucharist that side altars are now less valued than formerly. A separate chapel for small, weekday celebrations is one thing, but a side altar in a church is another. Current thought on this subject is expressed succinctly by Marion Hatchett in these words: "There should be only one altar in the room."

Despite this, there still remains a practical use for separate chapels, both from the point of view of making eucharists with small congregations more obviously corporate and for energy conservation, for it is much less expensive to heat a small chapel during the week than to heat a large church for the comfort of a dozen or so communicants at daily eucharists.

STAINED-GLASS WINDOWS

Although the art of coloring glass is of great antiquity, it was introduced into England no earlier than A.D. 680 when St. Benedict Biscop sent to Gaul for glaziers to make windows for this new monasteries at Wearmouth and Jarrow. Not long afterwards, St. Wilfred did the same for his minster at York. The windows probably consisted of small pieces of colored glass leaded together. Windows with biblical scenes and figures of saints came later—near the end of the twelfth century.

The earliest surviving examples are crude by later standards. They consisted of about fifty pieces of glass to the square foot, and the glass was thick and uneven in quality and deeply dyed. But considerable progress was made in the next several centuries, and by the end of the Middle Ages the art reached a high level of excellence.

As the Gothic age gave way to later styles, the ideals of rich color and simple treatment were abandoned. As more light was required—perhaps in part as a result of the invention of printing and the appearance of the English *Book of Common Prayer*—more and more clear glass was used in church windows, reducing the colored portions to heraldic bearings and other designs that occupied only a fraction of the window. Colored-glass windows became even less frequent in Wren churches. When used at all, they were often not stained-glass windows but merely representations on glass of oil paintings. By then most new churches—including all colonial ones—had clear glass windows, which went well with Georgian architecture.

But the Ecclesiologists, who arose after 1839, loved medieval ways and sought to revive Gothic settings for Anglican worship. Along with deep chancels, rood screens, stone altars, and credence tables, they inspired a revival of stained-glass windows. By the second half of the nineteenth century the revival was underway, but it was a long time before the glassmakers caught the true spirit of the medieval art, and it was not until the twentieth century that the revival reached its apogee.

The appearance of new styles of church architecture after World War I and the virtual cessation of building in Gothic Revival style after World War II has been matched by new and bold designs for stained-glass windows. Among the most notable examples are the windows in Le Corbusier's Pilgrimage Chapel at Ronchamp, France and in the new Coventry Cathedral in England.

With modern lighting there is little need for natural light filtering through window glass. Hence, stained glass today serves the practical purpose of protecting worshipers from the glare of too much natural light as well as the aesthetic one of providing beauty, color, and symbolism. That means, in many instances, that the stained-glass windows may once again be deeply dyed as they were in the high Middle Ages.

In view of the fact that contemporary church interiors are often somewhat colorless, richly colored glass, along with altar hangings and eucharistic vestments, can be used to provide much needed color. This can be achieved for relatively small expenditures by the use of non-objective designs, i.e., without figures or symbols, yet add great warmth to an otherwise pallid interior and reduce the glare of sunshine that otherwise would require the use of shutters or curtains.

STATIONS OF THE CROSS

The use of Stations of the Cross is said to have originated more than fifteen centuries ago as a result of (1) the visit to Jerusalem (c. 326) of St. Helena, the mother of the Emperor Constantine, (2) her attempts to find the holy places associated with our Lord's Passion and crucifixion, and (3) the subsequent custom of Christian pilgrims venerating the Stations of the Cross—especially in Holy Week. Upon their return home, they would naturally share their experience with their fellow parishioners and repeat the procedure each year.

By the late Middle Ages a series of pictures or carvings, designed for devotional purposes, appeared in many churches. They depicted incidents in our Lord's journey along the Via Dolorosa from Pilate's house to Calvary and were usually placed on the walls of the nave where they became the focus of popular devotion, especially during Lent and Passiontide. The Franciscans, in particular, are credited with popularizing the stations and encouraging the devotions.

Originally the number of stations varied widely. The final selection of fourteen episodes was not settled until the nineteenth century by which time there was an inclusion of several legendary or at least nonscriptural ones such as St. Veronica offering her headcloth to our Lord to wipe the blood and sweat from his face while carrying his cross to Calvary. This legend is first found in its present form in the fourteenth century, although there are earlier references to her. The Welsh historian Giraldus Cambrensis (1147–1223) told how the cloth, when returned to her by our Lord, had his facial features imprinted on it. Giraldus applied the word *veronica,* meaning "true image," to the cloth. Later, of course, it was transferred to the nameless woman, and she became known as St. Veronica.

Although this passiontide devotion seems to have played little or no part in the ethos of the English church from the sixteenth century until its revival by the Ecclesiologists and Ritualists in Victorian days, it deserves more general use than it now enjoys, for it is based largely on Holy Scripture. It is especially appropriate for Holy Week and can claim an impressively long history in Christian devotion. Two other benefits that attend its use are that it affords artists and woodcarvers an additional opportunity to embellish church interiors and it provides an additional audio-visual means of familiarizing the rising generation with biblical narratives.

Of the fourteen incidents upon which the Roman Catholic authorities finally settled less than two centuries ago, eight are based directly on events recorded in the gospels. The remaining six (numbers 3, 4, 6, 7, 9, and 13) are based on inferences from the Gospel narratives or, as in the case of St. Veronica, on pious legend.

Now that memorial tablets are out of fashion, the walls of many churches are often austere and colorless except for stained-glass windows. One way of decorating them and introducing a welcome touch of texture or color, as well as to take advantage of an ancient type of Christian devotion involving a dramatic pointing up of an important part of Holy Scripture, is to introduce Stations of the Cross, which may be carved, painted, or represented in tapestry or embroidery. If one has scruples about including non-scriptural episodes, there is nothing to prevent omitting them and using only the eight incidents that are explicit in the gospels. If they are to be used as a focus of a public service, however, it should be on weekdays in Lent. It should never displace the proper liturgy of Good Friday.

The Standing Liturgical Commissions' *Book of Occasional Services, 1979* includes an admirable service entitled "The Way of the Cross" (pages 55–71), covering all fourteen stations, that should recommend itself to Anglicans and pave the way for a more widespread revival of a devotion that has helped many Christians over the centuries to glory in the cross.

TABLETS OF THE LAW

A number of surviving eighteenth-century churches retain their "tablets of the law," and a few modern churches built in Georgian style have installed them, partly for the sake of propriety and partly as a means of embellishing church interiors.

There are a few instances of the use of tablets containing the Decalogue in English churches antedating the Reformation, but their use did not become general until the reign of Queen Elizabeth I. In 1560, two years after her accession, she instructed the Commissioners in Matters Ecclesiastical to see that tablets containing the Ten Commandments were set up in all churches in the realm, not only to be read for edification but also for ornamentation or, as she put it, to give "some comely ornament, and a demonstration that the church is a place of religion and prayer."[*]

When medieval canon law was recodified in England by the convocations of Canterbury and York in 1604, the eighty-second of the canons ordered "that the Ten Commandments be set upon the East ende of every church and chappell where the people may best see and reade the Same." Although only the Decalogue was specified, the general practice in both England and the American colonies was to place tablets containing the Apostles' Creed and the Lord's Prayer (often called the paternoster) alongside the tablet containing the Ten Commandments (or Decalogue).

In the colonies, the most common form of reredos (or "altar-piece," as they called it) was a panel or panels containing the

---

[*]Addleshaw & Etchells *The Architectural Setting of Anglican Worship* London: Faber and Faber, 1948, 28-29.

tablets, set between pilasters or other decorative work, the whole constituting the reredos. But there are a number of instances, especially when there was an east window behind and above the altar, in which the tablets were placed on either side of the window or altarpiece. Christ Church, Philadelphia, has them on the side walls of the chancel because of its large east window. A rarer departure from the norm is St. Paul's Church, Eastchester, New York, where they are on the south wall of the nave over the pulpit.

There was variety in both design and color, judging from surviving examples, but it is fair to say that the most common color was gold lettering on a black tablet. St. Michael's, Charleston, originally had tablets that were blue with gold lettering, however, and St. James', in Goose Creek, South Carolina, has tablets of white with dark lettering. The oldest known survivals are four painted canvas panels in the reredos of King's Chapel, Boston. They are gold on black and were painted in England in 1696 for the predecessor of the present church. The same color is used in those of St. Andrew's, Charleston (1706) and in St. Paul's, Wickford, Rhode Island (1707), although in the latter case, the creed and Lord's Prayer, which were probably added later, are black lettering on a white background. In Virginia, Christ Church, Lancaster County (1732), has black on white. And in Maryland, the same is true of St. James', Herring Creek (1765). Numerically they are exceptional. Most colonial churches in the two Chesapeake colonies used the more traditional gold on black.

Considering the fact that eighteenth-century churches were not as well lighted as are present-day ones, it is surprising that surviving tablets often do not have lettering sufficiently large to read, even with modern spectacles, from the nave. Possibly they were valued more as ornaments and symbols, i.e., to give "some comely ornament and a demonstration that the church is a place of religion and prayer," than for the practical purpose of being read by worshipers who lacked prayerbooks.

VESTMENTS

In general, vestments were developed from the everyday dress of the late Greco-Roman citizen: a tunic worn indoors and a chasuble or overgarment for outdoor wear. Together with the stole, these constituted eucharistic vestments by the ninth century or earlier. When the church penetrated into colder climates than it had known in Mediterranean lands, the clergy took to wearing a fur garment under their tunica alba. To make the tightfitting alb large enough to be put easily over the pelliceum (as the fur garment was called), it was made fuller and given wide sleeves. This "super pelliceum" became the surplice, which since the twelfth century has been the distinctive habit of the lower clergy and has been used by priests for sacraments other than the eucharist. Bishops took to wearing rochets rather than surplices and, of course, mitres. Copes were processional vestments for bishops and priests alike. There appeared a variety of other vestments, such as almuces, dalmatics, and tunicles, that usually indicated rank. Copes and chasubles were often made of rich materials in the Middle Ages, and albs and amices and maniples were often ornamented with apparels of damask or embroidery.

An instance of liturgical change requiring alterations in the design of vestments can be seen in the late medieval ceremonial of elevating the host after the consecration in the eucharist. This was difficult to do while wearing a large, embroidered chasuble of early medieval design. The greater emphasis on the host after the institution of the Feast of Corpus Christi in 1264 resulted in the elevation, and that, in turn, resulted in chasubles being cut away at the sides to facilitate the ceremonial action. In time, of course, it produced the "fiddleback" variety, which was little more than a strip of colored matterial hanging down in front and in back of the celebrant.

Another instance has to do with the decoration of chasubles. In earlier centuries when priests celebrated from behind free-standing altars, there was no reason to decorate the back of the chasuble more than the front. But in the Middle Ages when celebrants habitually faced the east, the backs of chasubles came to be more richly decorated. With the revival of freestanding altars and westward celebrations, however, the situation has been reversed again, and modern chasubles often avoid favoring the back over the front.

The Reformation greatly reduced the variety of vestments used in England. Bishops continued to wear rochets and copes, used mitres, which were often carried in hand rather than worn on the head. Copes were worn at the eucharist in cathedrals and collegiate churches and for royal coronations. Albs and chasubles were largely disused, although they survived in a few locations. In general, parish priests wore only a surplice over their cassocks, surmounted by a hood and tippet. For street habit, they wore a cassock and cincture surmounted by a gown and tippet. The canons of 1604 mandated a square cap—now called a Cranmer or Canterbury cap—which is the late medieval form of what Roman Catholics call a biretta. By the eighteenth century, however, most priests in England and America had substituted the three-cornered hat of the period for the canonical square cap. Later, when modern coats replaced gowns and the cassock was cut off at the waist for convenience in riding horses, the seventeenth-century street habit became today's familiar clerical attire.

In the seventeenth century, the Puritans abhorred the surplice as a "rag of popery," that is, an unwarranted vestige of the corrupt medieval church. Later, when their rancor was moderated by the rising toleration of the Age of Reason, they still disliked it and sometimes dubbed the surplice a "Canterbury nightgown." Originally ankle-length and very full, the surplice was progressively shortened. In Roman Catholic churches by the eighteenth century it barely reached the waist and had short sleeves. In this abbreviated form it is known as a "cotta." The Roman clergy trimmed it with lace from the sixteenth century onwards.

In Anglican use it remained long and full, but when the clergy took to wearing wigs in emulation of their lay brethren, the surplice was slit down the front and provided with buttons, so that the priest could put it on and take it off in the chancel, in full view of the congregation, without disarraying his wig. After the reverend gentlemen gave up wearing wigs some decades after they had gone out of fashion, the surplice gradually regained its historic form without front opening or buttons. But the revived, ancient form did not last long. With the coming of the Industrial Revolution and mass production, the surplice soon fell victim to competition between clerical tailors who, in the interests of saving expense, progressively reduced the once comely garment to the short, skimpy "sausage skin" variety that was all too common several generations ago. As a result of the popularity of Percy Dearmer's *Parson's Handbook* and the influence of the Liturgical Movement, the surplice has once again recovered its original length and fullness.

The Catholic Revival, ushered in by the Tractarians in a doctrinal sense, was picked up and translated into ceremonial enrichment by the Ritualists, who, like their allies the Ecclesiologists, were caught up in a rapture when it came to medieval precedents. Needless to say, they reintroduced many medieval vestments that had long been disused. Despite the entrenched opposition of the Evangelicals, they succeeded to a remarkable degree in making beautifully embroidered stoles, apparelled albs and amices, and richly decorated chasubles widely accepted and widely used throughout the Anglican Communion. But details as to their design were grounds for disagreement. The Alcuin Club buffs and the Dearmerites, armed with a growing library of scholarly and documented studies, strove mightily to have them authentically made from medieval English designs rather than ignorantly copied from the baroque forms, which they regarded as decadent but which were in use among Roman Catholics. Their adversaries of the Society of SS. Peter and Paul took the opposite point of view and favored the emulation of contemporary Roman use in every detail, arguing that this is what Anglican use would have become had there been no Reformation.

The same impulse that produced the new Coventry Cathedral and countless other new-style churches has also invaded the realm of vestment design and has produced an extravaganza of impressive chasubles and stoles of varying degrees of artistic excellence. Some of them, although stunning because of their bold design, color, and texture, seem more appropriate to the ambiance of contemporary architecture than to Romanesque, Gothic, or Georgian churches.

Since World War II, the appearance of the "cassock-alb" and its widespread use by Roman Catholics and Lutherans as well as Anglicans has made it the quintessential ecumenical vestment. It is often used with a stole but without a chasuble—which is a blessing in hot weather. It is possible that this garment, especially if it is white and has large sleeves, will eventually replace not only the old, tightfitting alb and amice but the surplice as well, for it can be worn with a hood and tippet at choir offices and with a stole for administering sacraments. The variety that is full and long and has wide sleeves resembles the eighteenth-century form of the surplice and therefore is particularly appropriate in Georgian churches. One further advantage is that it is much less expensive than a well-made cassock and a long and full surplice, which is an important consideration nowadays for a seminarian and a newly ordained priest. But the frequent swing of the pendulum in times past, with respect to vestments and almost every other material accompaniment of worship, prevents even the wisest of observers from predicting the precise details of future change with any degree of confidence.

Farewell to the Reader

Remember, the supreme wonder of the history of the Christian Church is that always in moments when it has seemed most dead out of its own body there has sprung up new life; so that in age after age it has renewed itself, and age after age by its renewal has carried the world forward into new stages of progress, as it will do in our day, if only we give ourselves in devotion to its Lord and take our place in its service.*

Archbishop William Temple (1881-1944)

---

*Hugh C. Warner: *Daily Readings From William Temple*, London: Hodder & Stoughton, 1948, 28-29.

Illustrations

FIGURE 1

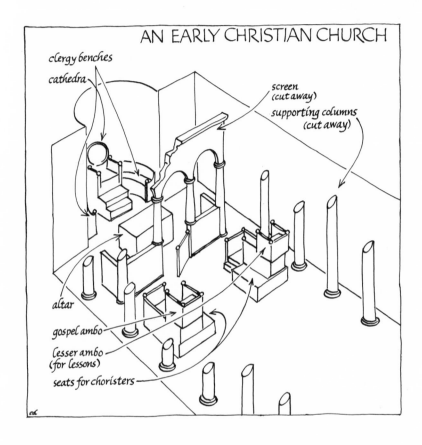

AN EARLY CHRISTIAN CHURCH

clergy benches
cathedra
screen
(cut away)
supporting columns
(cut away)
altar
gospel ambo
lesser ambo
(for lessons)
seats for choristers

AN EARLY CHRISTIAN CHURCH. By the fourth century the common form of a church was that of a basilica, a type of building that had been developed by the Romans to house a court of justice. Entered by way of a forecourt and covered porch, it was rectangular in shape but with a projecting apse at the far end. The interior was characterized by a row of columns on each side and by a partition or screen that separated the altar area from the nave where the main body of worshipers assembled. Beyond the screen stood a freestanding altar, roughly cubical in shape. Behind it and somewhat elevated above the floor on which the altar stood were seats for the bishop and his attending priests and deacons.

The screen consisted of panels rising from the floor, perhaps four feet in height. Above it were slender columns that supported an architrave from which votive lamps might be suspended. Although the progenitor of the later rood screen in the West (and the iconostasis in the East), basilican screens were not solid, hence the altar could be seen from the nave. In front of the screen there were places for the choristers. Also, the altar was usually dignified by a ciborium, or architectural canopy, supported by four slender columns.

In the early days, the sermon was preached from the *cathedra*, or chair of the bishop, which stood in the center of the apse behind and a little above the altar. It was from this place that the bishop or, in his absence, the priest presided over the eucharist and preached the sermon. The gospel was read from an elevated platform called an *ambo* approached by a flight of steps and protected by a parapet. Located in front of the screen, it was larger than the later medieval pulpit because it had to accommodate not only the gospeler but also his attendant taperers. It was used on Easter Eve by the deacon who sang the *exsultet* at the blessing of the paschal candle (see page 286 of the 1979 Prayer Book). And from the steps of the ambo, part of the psalmody was sung by chanters between the reading of the epistle and the gospel. This came to be called the "gradual," from the Latin *gradus*, a step. Originally there was only one ambo, placed on the north side of the axis of the church. Later two were used; the second on the south side for lessons at the eucharist. To show greater honor to the Gospel, the one on the north was usually larger and more imposing than its counterpart on the south.

Baptismal fonts were not visible. They were consigned to separate buildings or rooms because in early Christian practice catechumens of both sexes and all ages were baptized in the nude. After their water baptism and chrismation, they were brought into the church for admission to the eucharist, which completed their Christian initiation.

Communion rails had not yet come into use. At the appropriate moment the gate to the altar was opened, and the priests and deacons came forth to administer Holy Communion to the people who came forward and stood to receive it.

FIGURE 2

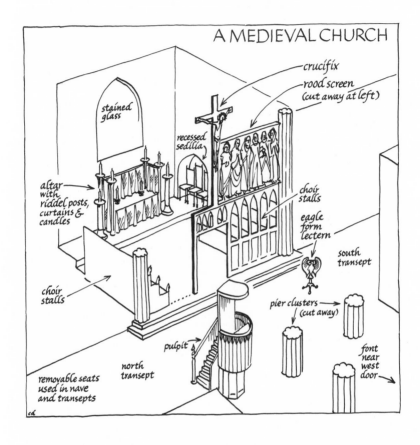

A MEDIEVAL CHURCH

crucifix
rood screen
(cut away at left)

stained glass

recessed sedilia

altar with riddel posts, curtains & candles

choir stalls

eagle form lectern

south transept

choir stalls

pier clusters (cut away)

pulpit

north transept

font near west door

removable seats used in nave and transepts

A MEDIEVAL CHURCH. Because of the great increase in the number of persons in Holy Orders and because of the proliferation of minor orders, the apsidal ends of Romanesque churches were deepened to make room for them. By the time Gothic architecture came into its own, the chancel had become a prominent feature of medieval churches. Meanwhile, the structural divider that visibly separated the chancel from the nave developed into the rood screen. Another development was the appearance of chapels, an outgrowth of the cult of saints, the custom of votive masses, and the belief that each priest should celebrate the eucharist every day and no two at the same altar.

For didactic purposes, symbolic importance was attached to the architectural setting of the eucharist. Gothic churches, often cruciform, were said to represent Christ on the cross. Their customary five doors, representing the wounds of our Lord, were often painted blood red. The nave, which held the people, stood for the world, "the Church militant." Hence, Holy Scripture was read and sermons preached there. This resulted in lecterns and pulpits being located in the nave. Now that candidates were no longer baptized in the nude, fonts were placed in the church itself, rather than in chapels or separate baptistries. They were commonly near the west door of the nave in order to point up the fact that entry into Christ's Church was by means of baptism.

The rood screen with its great crucifix symbolized the fact that our Lord's Passion and death alone gave the faithful admittance to paradise. The chancel, now enlarged to include the singers as well as the clergy, represented paradise. The white-robed choristers suggested the celestial choir of angels. The sanctuary with the high altar represented heaven itself and the heavenly banquet where the redeemed met and enjoyed the company of the ascended Lord. Thus the sanctuary symbolized a foretaste of salvation and a glimpse of eternal life.

Congregational participation declined because the liturgy continued to be in Latin long after the rise of modern languages and because the musical setting of worship was progressively elaborated so that it could no longer be sung by the people but only by trained choirs. The developing ceremonial suggested that the celebrant was speaking to God on behalf of the people and performing the eucharistic action for them rather than with them. Hence, instead of celebrating facing the people from behind the altar, the priest now stood in front of the altar with his back to the people, and altars instead of being freestanding were placed against the east wall. The earlier structural ciborium was now converted into a reredos with riddel posts and curtains and perhaps a tester high above the altar.

By the late Middle Ages the altar would likely have had two candlesticks on it as well as other lights on the riddels and around the altar, especially on great feasts. The altar itself, now much longer than in early Christian days, was covered by a fitted frontal of rich material, and there was a color sequence, which was elaborate or simple depending upon the ability of each cathedral, abbey, or parish church to obtain expensive furnishings.

FIGURE 3

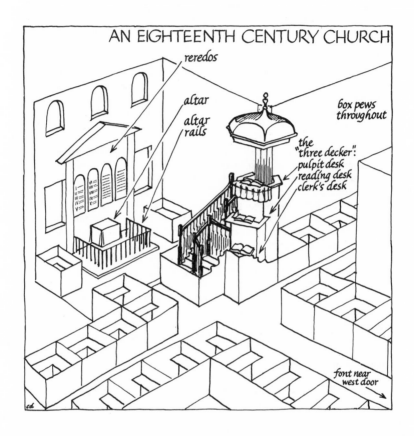

AN EIGHTEENTH CENTURY CHURCH

reredos

altar

altar rails

box pews throughout

the "three decker": pulpit desk reading desk clerk's desk

font near west door

AN EIGHTEENTH CENTURY CHURCH. The English reformers of the sixteenth century accepted the interior arrangement inherited from the medieval Church but undertook to correct the liturgical faults of the late Middle Ages by endeavoring to recover a sense of corporate worship. Archbishop Cranmer did this by creating the *Book of Common Prayer,* which simplified the services, translated them into English and provided congregational responses. He also engaged John Merbecke to adapt simple plainsong melodies to serve as settings for services on the principle of one note to each syllable. With these changes came a new emphasis upon hearing the liturgy, and that in turn created a demand for a different architectural setting for worship, designed to make churches more auditory. The change was accomplished chiefly by the great English architect, Sir Christopher Wren.

At first, the hearing of the services was facilitated by enjoining the priests to speak distinctly and in a loud voice and by moving much of the liturgical action from the far end of the deep chancel to places nearer the people. The portable wooden altars that replaced the medieval stone ones could be brought forward into the chancel for celebrationss. Matins, the litany, and the eucharist as far as the offertory were transferred to the nave in the interest of audibility. At the offertory, the priest, accompanied by those of his parishioners who intended to receive Holy Communion, went into the chancel where they could be close to the holy table, hear the consecration, and see the manual acts.

This shifting of the altar into the chancel was too much of a departure from medieval practice for High Church people such as Archbishop Laud and the Caroline divines. They initiated a partial Counter-Reformation that, after 1660, resulted in restoring altars to their accustomed place at the east end, and they required them to be fenced with altar rails to protect them from profane and irreverent use. They also revived the early Christian type of altar cloth, now known as Laudian or Jacobean frontals, that coexisted with the fitted type until banished by the Victorian Ecclesiologists.

The practice continued of having the entire Ministry of the Word in the nave. As in Elizabethan days, the priest and communicants went forward together to the altar at the offertory where they could be close to the celebrant for the consecration. As more of the service took place in the nave than had been the custom in the Middle Ages, pulpits became larger and were associated in the minds of the worshipers with the liturgy as well as with the sermon. Located in the nave, eighteenth-century pulpits often had a reading desk for the priest at a lower level and even another, at still a lower level, for the parish clerk, thus becoming the so-called "three-decker."

As time went on, the chancel screen that had survived the turmoil of the Reformation, went out of fashion in the eighteenth century, and the depth of the chancel was progressively reduced until, by the late eighteenth century, it was often omitted altogether. Thereafter the altar and the small area surrounded by the rails constituted all that was left of the medieval chancel. By then, however, it was adequate for the needs of the liturgical practice of the day. Unvested parish choirs were usually placed in the rear gallery, and there was a shortage of priests. Moreover, the day of such lay ministers as crucifers, taperers, thurifers, and chalicists had not yet dawned.

Fonts were still sometimes placed in their traditional location near the west door, but as time went on, the premium on space often resulted in their being transferred to the east end near the altar. The nave and transepts were filled with high box pews with doors, designed to retain heat from portable foot warmers. These continued in use as long as churches were unheated—well into the nineteenth century.

FIGURE 4

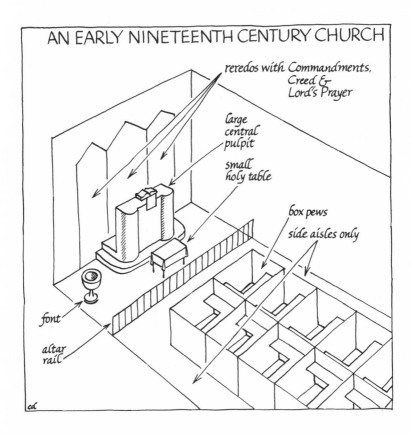

AN EARLY NINETEENTH CENTURY CHURCH. Many older churches passed through the early nineteenth century with there interiors unchanged, but the Evangelicals who reached their apex of influence in the early nineteenth century, and other church members who agreed with them about the setting of worship built or retrofitted churches that departed to an extreme degree from the received medieval arrangement. The auditory principle reached its apogee because their unprecedented emphasis on preaching led them to create church interiors that proclaimed their conviction that worship was less a matter of participation in an action than it was of speaking and hearing the Word. In extreme instances, Anglican worship had never been so completely intellectualized or so nearly stripped of ceremonial. On the other hand, the arrangement adopted, by bringing the altar and people close together, anticipated one of the objectives of the later Liturgical Movement.

When stoves began to be used for heating churches on Sundays, the old box pews that had come down from the colonial period were reduced in height or replaced by slip pews in order to facilitate radiation and convection, thereby enabling the congregation to listen to the long sermons in physical comfort.

Having no liturgical use for chancels, the Evangelicals abandoned them altogether, and they scrapped the traditional idea of having three distinct liturgical centers. Instead, they combined pulpit, altar, and font to make a single focus of worship at the front of the church. The pulpit was placed in the middle of the east end with an inconspicuous holy table in front of and below it. Pulpits lost their graceful, wine glass shape and resembled a magistrate's desk, visually dominating the interior and overpowering the altar. Instead of a stone font, as required by English canon law, or a separate wooden structure to support a baptismal bowl, the Evangelicals usually preferred a small silver bowl placed on the holy table when there were baptisms.

Having little enthusiasm for liturgical processions, the Evangelicals generally eliminated central aisles and filled the body of the church with blocks of pews. As a result, the interiors of many early nineteenth century Anglican churches were scarcely distinguishable from those of the Congregationalists, Presbyterians, and Baptists.

FIGURE 5

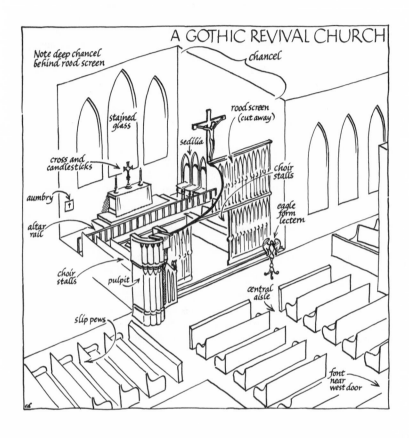

A GOTHIC REVIVAL CHURCH. Touched off by John Keble's sermon "National Apostasy" in 1833, the Oxford Movement began to leaven the Anglican church and bring about a Catholic revival similar to, but far more complete than, that of the Caroline divines in the seventeenth century. Largely theological at first, it eventually spilled over into the realm of liturgy and therefore produced an architectural expression. The Ritualists sought to revive medieval ceremonial and the Ecclesiologists promoted Gothic Revival architecture. Aided by the Romantic movement in literature and especially by the popular novels of Sir Walter Scott, the two groups were remarkably successful in their attempt to revive the medieval splendor of the English church.

The Ecclesiologists insisted on a particular phase of Gothic—that of the "decorated" style that flourished from 1260 to 1360—as being the only proper model for Anglican churches. Also, they recovered the idea that a church should have three distinct liturgical centers and that it should have a deep chancel visibly separated from the nave, preferably by a rood screen.

The Ecclesiologists abhorred the eighteenth-century "three-deckers" and replaced them with medieval-style pulpits and separate lecterns, usually on the opposite side of the central aisle from the pulpit. Fonts were once more made of stone as they had been in the Middle Ages, and they were placed near the west door as they had been formerly. Central blocks of pews were removed, central aisles restored, and box pews replaced by slip pews after the medieval fashion. Other visible changes favored by the Ecclesiologists included the use of stained-glass widows, aumbries or pyxes for the Reserved Sacrament, and the recovery of medieval vestments and paraphernalia that were believed to have been in use in English churches in "the second year of the reign of Edward VI," i.e., between January 28, 1548 and January 27, 1549, as had been authorized by the ornaments rubric of the 1662 Prayer Book.

The revival of medieval ways brought additional ministers to the altar, specifically a deacon and subdeacon in addition to the priest. Instead of a chair on each side of the altar, medieval sedilia were restored. Chancels were in vogue again and often had to be deepened in order to accommodate vested choirs and other functionaries such as crucifers, taperers, and thurifers that had not been much in evidence since the sixteenth century.

FIGURE 6

A CONTEMPORARY SETTING

choir seating

sedilia

combination lectern-pulpit

pavement lights

portable font

altar

A CONTEMPORARY SETTING. As the objectives of the Liturgical Movement are to recover the concept of the eucharist as a corporate action involving both priests and people and to restore more fully the active participation of the people in worship, changes have been made in church interiors that involve going behind the neomedievalism of the Ecclesiologists to the practice of early Christian times. This, in turn, has resulted in the building of new churches that reflect the insights of the Liturgical Movement and in refitting existing churches along similar lines. Many older churches, especially those built before 1840, that had been rearranged later to meet the standards of the Ecclesiologists were rearranged once more. The architectural axiom "form follows function" is as true today as at any time since the early Christians emerged from hiding and built churches designed to house their liturgical practices.

Altars have been brought forward from the east wall and placed at the front of the chancel or at the head of the nave. Now that they were freestanding, it was once more possible for priests to celebrate from behind them, facing the people. This change rendered impractical the continued use of an altar cross, which had become virtually universal in Anglican churches. The vanished altar cross has sometimes been replaced by reviving the medieval practice of placing a processional cross in a socket behind the celebrant's chair.

Existing rood screens have been demolished or made to serve as reredoses for nave altars. Deep chancels filled with choir stalls that separated the people in the nave from the priest at the altar have become anathema. In some cases, the choristers remain in what had been the chancel but behind rather than in front of the sanctuary or altar area. In other cases, organs and choirs have been relocated, as formerly, in west galleries.

This rearrangement not only brings the altar and the people close together but also provides a spacious setting for the altar, more adequate seating accommodations for the celebrant and other clergy behind the altar as in early Christian days, and additional room for the host of new attendants that have become widespread in recent years—lectors, chalicists, and banner bearers.

In current liturgical practice, fonts have acquired a new importance, because baptism is now regarded as a regular part of the principal eucharists on certain Sundays and holy days each year, rather than being consigned to hours outside the principal services. There is, therefore, a new imperative to place the font in a conspicuous location where it can best be seen by the congregation and also to position it so that the priest can stand behind it, facing the people. In some cases this may mean that it will be at the east end, near the altar, rather than in its traditional place near the west door. The governing principle, however, is the convenience of the people, who are expected to participate in the baptismal action no less than in that of the eucharist.

Glossary

For more complete information the reader is referred to any of various dictionaries, especially F. L. Cross, ed., *The Oxford Dictionary of the Christian Church* (1957) and subsequent editions, from which many of the following definitions are drawn.

AMBO   In Christian basilicas, a raised platform of wood or stone from which Scriptures, litanies, and other public parts of the liturgy were read to the people. Approached by stairs, it was surmounted by a parapet and provided with a desk to hold the liturgical book. Larger than the later pulpit, the ambo was designed to accommodate not only the lector but also his attendant taperers. Originally there was only one in each church, but later a second was added. The larger one on the north side was for reading the gospel; the smaller one on the south side for reading the other lessons. In the course of the Middle Ages, the ambo was replaced by the smaller pulpit. Recently, there has been a tendency in some places to reintroduce the ambo.

APSE   A semicircular or polygonal eastern end to a chancel.

AUMBRY   A locked cupboard or safe in the wall of a church or sacristy to hold sacred books and vessels, relics, and the reserved sacrament. There is a question how widespread it was in medieval England, but it was revived by the Victorian Ecclesiologists because it was of medieval origin.

BAROQUE   The ornate style of art and architecture that flourished in Italy during the seventeenth and early eighteenth centuries and spread throughout the continent, especially France, Spain, and Austria. Its lofty grandeur and richness of decoration infused new life and religious feeling into the cold correctness of the later Renaissance. See also Rococo.

BASILICA   A type of building developed by the Romans to house a court of justice. After the fourth century, it was adopted by the church to house its liturgical action.

CATHEDRA   A bishop's chair or throne in his cathedral, which takes its name from the cathedra it houses.

CIBORIUM   (1) An architectural canopy supported by four slender columns to dignify the altar; (2) A chalice-shaped vessel, with a lid or cover, that contains the bread of the eucharist. It came into use early in the Middle Ages.

DOOM   A depiction of the Last Judgment with our Lord separating the redeemed from the lost souls. In medieval churches the doom was usually located on the tympanum or wooden boarding that filled in the chancel arch over the rood loft.

DORSAL or DOSSAL   A piece of cloth, often embroidered, that hangs behind an altar in lieu of a reredos.

ENCAUSTIC TILES   Tiles used to pave medieval sanctuaries and chancels, decorated with patterns in different colored clays, inlaid in brick and fired. The technique was revived by the Ecclesiologists, and the product used in Gothic Revival churches.

EXSULTET   The paschal (i.e., Easter) proclamation or paschal praise sung by the deacon at the blessing of the paschal candle on Easter Eve. See 1979 *Book of Common Prayer,* page 286.

GOTHIC ARCHITECTURE   The style of building in Europe from the thirteenth through the fifteenth centuries, characterized by the pointed arch and vault. The use of diagonal ribs to support and strengthen the groined vaults helped create an independent skeleton frame for the vault masonry that rested on vertical piers, rather than on the walls. Hence the walls, no longer needed for support, became thinner and were pierced by large windows. Revived during the second half of the nineteenth century, it has left its mark on many churches and academic buildings.

GRADINE   (see under RETABLE)

HEARSE LIGHTS   A name applied to, *inter alia,* the standing candlesticks that flank a coffin at the burial office.

MONSTRANCE   A vessel, usually of precious metal, used for exposing the eucharistic Host for veneration. When the cultus of the Blessed Sacrament spread in the later Middle Ages, the Host was contained in a closed ciborium. In the sixteenth century, the bowl was elongated and provided with a glass window through which the sacred contents could be seen by the worshipers.

PAROUSIA   A Greek word meaning "presence" or "arrival." In its English form, it denotes the future return of Christ in glory, i.e., the Second Coming, to judge the living and the dead.

PELAGIAN HERESY   A theological system that takes its name from a fifth-century British (or Irish) lay monk named Pelagius who settled in Rome and acquired a reputation for learning. His system was attacked by St. Augustine and subsequently condemned by virtually the whole Church. It held that people take the initial and fundamental steps towards salvation by their own efforts, apart from God's grace.

PYX   A container for the Reserved Sacrament that was suspended over or in front of the altar. Often of precious metal, it was sometimes wrought in the shape of a dove. Common in medieval England, the pyx was revived by the nineteenth-century Ecclesiologists along with the aumbry.

REREDOS   Any decoration above and behind an altar but usually confined to solid structures of stone or wood that are carved and painted (as opposed to dorsals, which are of cloth).

RETABLE or GRADINE   A shelf or ledge above and behind an altar on which the cross, lights, ornaments, and flowers are placed. It appeared in the sixteenth century and continued in use until recently. Percy Dearmer and his followers execrated it as a corrupt addition to a proper liturgical altar. The Liturgical Movement with its emphasis on freestanding altars is rapidly doing away with retables.

RIDDELS   Curtains at the north and south ends of an altar, suspended from rods that connect the riddel posts; these posts were often richly polychromed and sometimes surmounted by candles known as riddel lights, in the Middle Ages. They were revived in the second half of the nineteenth century.

ROCOCO   An eighteenth-century development of baroque architecture and decoration that originated in France and spread widely in Europe, especially in Roman Catholic countries. It lasted from about 1715 to about 1750 and was characterized by excessive, but graceful, ornateness.

ROMANESQUE (or NORMAN) ARCHITECTURE   The name given to the architectural style that prevailed throughout Europe from the eleventh to the thirteenth centuries, characterized by the use of round arches and massive stone vaulting. Compared with the later Gothic style, Romanesque churches were generally distinguished by massiveness and simplicity. In England, the style is known as Norman because it was introduced after the Norman conquest in 1066.

ROOD, ROOD SCREEN, ROOD LOFT   A crucifix or cross, often with the attendant figures of the Blessed Virgin Mary and St. John. A rood was commonly placed upon the chancel screen in the Middle Ages, for which reason the screen came to be called a rood screen, or upon a beam across the chancel arch known as a rood beam. A gallery built above the rood screen to accommodate an organ and choristers was called a rood loft.

SACRAMENT HOUSE   A late medieval variant of the aumbry in Germany, Belgium, and France. The sacrament house was a tall, shrine-like receptacle for the Reserved Sacrament, usually in the form of a small tower, the central part of which was done in open work, and often ornate, with carved reliefs representing the Last Supper, the Passion, and related subjects. After the sixteenth century it was largely replaced by the tabernacles.

SACRING or SANCTUS BELL   A small bell rung inside a church or a large one rung from the church tower at the elevation of the host in the mass. Used in England at least as early as 1240, its rationale was to call the people's attention to the most important part of the eucharistic action. The outside bell was used, according to Archbishop Peckham in 1281, to enable those who were working in the field or at home to participate to the extent of genuflecting and offering a silent prayer at the moment of consecration.

SANCTUARY   The area around an altar, specifically the area within the altar rails. It may not with propriety be applied to the entire church interior.

TABERNACLE   A box set in the middle of the altar to hold the reserved species. Tabernacles became popular in Roman Catholic use after the sixteenth century and were virtually unknown in England until they were introduced by the Victorian Ecclesiologists, who mistakenly thought them to be medieval in origin.

TETRAGRAMMATON   A technical term for the four-letter Hebrew word for God, JHVH. Because of its sacred character, the Jews avoided uttering it when reading the Scriptures aloud and substituted *Adonai,* the Hebrew word for "Lord." To call attention to the substitution, in Hebrew manuscripts the vowel-points of *Adonai* were inserted into the four consonants of the tetragrammaton. Since the sixteenth century, the bastard word

"Jehovah," obtained by fusing the two, has been widely used. It is now thought that the original pronunciation of the tetragrammaton is represented in English by "Yahweh."

THURIBLE, THURIFER A metal vessel for the ceremonial burning of incense. Commonly it is suspended by chains from which it can be swung in procession and used to cense persons and objects. The person who carries the thurible is known as a thurifer.

Bibliography

Addleshaw, G. W. O. *The High Church Tradition: A Study in the Liturgical Thought of the Seventeenth Century.* London: Faber and Faber Ltd., 1941.

Addleshaw, G. W. O., and Etchells, Frederick. *The Architectural Setting of Anglican Worship: An Inquiry into the Arrangements for Public Worship in the Church of England from the Reformation to the Present Day.* London: Faber and Faber Ltd., 1950.

Anglican Society in Great Britain since 1926, in North America since 1932. Quarterly periodicals: *The Anglican Catholic* (England), *The Anglican* (America).

Anson, Peter F. *Fashions in Church Furnishings, 1840–1940.* London: Faith Press, 1960.

Associated Parishes. Offers various publications relating to particular services in the Prayer Book.

Atchley, E. G. Cuthbert. *A History of the Use of Incense in Divine Worship.* Alcuin Club Collections XIII. London: Longmans, Green and Co., 1909.

Betts, Darby Wood, ed. *Architecture and the Church.* Greenwich CT: Joint Commission on Architecture and the Allied Arts, Seabury Press, 1960.

Book of Occasional Services. New York: The Church Hymnal Corporation, 1979.

Central Council for the Care of Churches. *Churches and Their Furnishings: Fifteenth Report of the Central Council for the Care of Churches.* Westminster, S. W. I.: Church House, 1961.

Clayton, H. J. *Cassock and Gown.* Alcuin Club Tracts XVIII. London: Oxford University Press, 1929.

Constitution and Canons Ecclesiastical, 1604. London: Oxford University Press, 1923.

Constitution on the Liturgy. Promulgated by Pope Paul VI, Second Vatican Council, December 4, 1963. Washington: National Catholic Welfare Conference, 1964.

Cope, Gilbert. *Ecclesiology Then and Now: A few more words to Church Builders.* London: Ecclesiological Society, 1963.

Cope, Gilbert, ed. *Making the Building Serve the Liturgy.* London: A. R. Mowbray, 1962.

Cox, J. Charles. *English Church Fittings, Furniture and Accessories.* New York and London: G. P. Putnam Sons, and B. T. Batsford Ltd., 1923.

———. *The English Parish Church: An Account of the Chief Building Types and of Their Materials During Nine Centuries.* London and New York: B. T. Batsford Ltd., and Charles Scribners Sons, 1914.

Cox, J. Charles, and Harvey, Alfred. *English Church Furniture.* London: Methuer & Co., 1907.

Cross, F. L., ed. *The Oxford Dictionary of the Christian Church.* London: Oxford University Press, 1957.

Crossley, Fred H. *English Church Craftsmanship: An Introduction to the Work of the Mediaeval Period and Some Account of Later Developments.* London: B. T. Batsford Ltd., 1941.

Davies, J. G. *The Architectural Setting of Baptism.* London: Barrie & Rockliff, 1962.

———. *The Origin and Development of Early Christian Architecture.* London: SCM Press, 1952.

Davies, J. G., ed. *A Dictionary of Liturgy and Worship.* London: SCM Press, 1972.

Davis, Vernon Perdue, and Rawlings, James Scott. *The Colonial Churches of Virginia, Maryland and North Carolina: Their Interiors and Worship.* Richmond: Dietz Press, 1985.

Dearmer, Percy. *The Parson's Handbook: containing Practical Directions Both for Parsons and others as to the Management of The Parish Church and its Services according to the Anglican*

Use, as set forth in the Book of Common Prayer. 12th edition. London: Geoffrey Cumberlege, 1932.

Dendy, D. R. *The Use of Lights in Christian Worship.* Alcuin Club Collections XLI. London: SPCK, 1959.

Dix, Dom Gregory. *The Shape of the Liturgy.* London: Dacre Press, 1945.

Dorsey, Stephen P. *Early English Churches in America, 1607-1807.* New York: Oxford University Press, 1952.

Freestone, W. H. *The Sacrament Reserved: A Survey of the Practice of Reserving the Eucharist, with special Reference to the Communion of the Sick, during the first twelve centuries.* Alcuin Club Collections XXI. London: A. R. Mowbray, 1917.

Gilchrist, James. *Anglican Church Plate.* London: The Connoisseur and Michael Joseph, 1967.

Glendenning, F. J., ed. *The Church and the Arts.* London: SCM Press, 1960.

Hammond, Peter. *Liturgy and Architecture.* New York: Columbia University Press, 1961.

Hatchett, Marion J. "Architectural Implications of the Book of Common Prayer 1979." *Occasional Papers of the Standing Liturgical Commission* (December 1984). Reprinted in *The Anglican* (Winter 1984) and in the Associated Parishes' *Open* (August 1985).

"Old Anglican Texts and Customs Revived in the Proposed Book of Common Prayer." *The Anglican* (Spring, 1977).

Hope, William St. John, and Atchley, E. G. Cuthbert. *English Liturgical Colours.* London: SPCK, 1918.

Legg, J. Wickham, ed. *English Church Life from the Restoration to the Tractarian Movement: Considered in Some of its Neglected or Forgotten Features.* London: Longmans, Green and Co., 1914.

Lockett, William, ed. *The Modern Architectural Setting of The Liturgy.* London: SPCK, 1962.

McAllister, James L., Jr. "Architecture and Change in the Diocese of Virginia." (Episcopal Church) *Historical Magazine* 45 (September 1976): 297-323.

Middleton, Arthur Pierce. "Liturgical Change with or without Prayer Book Revision." *The Anglican* (Fall 1987): 4-12.

Middleton, Arthur Pierce. "Liturgical Space and the New Prayer Book." *The Anglican* (Fall 1980): 2-4.

———. "Observations of a Latter-Day Ecclesiologist." *The Anglican* (Spring 1984): 2-6.

Norris, Herbert. *Church Vestments: The Origin and Development.* New York: E. P. Dutton, 1950.

Ollard, S. L.; Grosse, Gordon; and Bond, Maurice F. *A Dictionary of English Church History.* Revised edition. New York and London: Morehouse-Gorham and A. R. Mowbray, 1948.

Oman, Charles. *English Church Plate, 597-1830.* London: 1957.

Pocknee, Cyril E. *Cross and Crucifix: In Christian Worship and Devotion.* Alcuin Club Tracts XXXII. London: A. R. Mowbray, 1962.

———. *Liturgical Vesture: Its Origins and Development.* Alcuin Club Tracts XXX. London: A. R. Mowbray, 1960.

———. *The Christian Altar: In History and Today.* Alcuin Club. London: A. R. Mowbray, 1963.

Rose, Harold Wickliffe. *The Colonial Houses of Worship in America: Built in the English Colonies before the Republic, 1607-1789, and Still Standing.* New York: Hastings House, 1963.

Shands. Alfred R. *The Liturgical Movement and the Local Church.* London: SCM Press, 1959.

Shepherd, Massey Hamilton, Jr. "At All Times and in All Places." Greenwich, CT: Seabury Press, 1953.

Sherman, Jonathan G., ed. *Church Buildings and Furnishings.* Greenwich, CT: Joint Commission on Architecture and the Allied Arts, Seabury Press, 1958.

Srawley, J. H. *The Liturgical Movement: Its Origin and Growth.* London: A. R. Mowbray, 1954.

Staley, Vernon, ed. *Hierurgia Anglicana: Documents and Extracts Illustrative of The Ceremonial of the Anglican Church after the Reformation.* Edited originally by members of the Ecclesiological Late Cmabridge Camden Society, 1848, three volumes. London: The De La More Press, 1902-1904.

Stanton, Phoebe B. *The Gothic Revival and American Church Architecture.* Baltimore: 1968.

Upton, Dell. *Holy Things and Profane: Anglican Parish Churches in Colonial Virginia.* Cambridge, Mass.: *The Architectural History Foundation,* New York, MIT Press, 1986.

Virginia Museum. "Church Silver of Colonial Virginia." Richmond: The Virginia Museum, 1970.

Virginia State Library, Richmond. Series of published vestry books of colonial Virginia parishes.

The Warham Guild Handbook: Historical and Descriptive Notes on "Ornaments of the Church and of the Ministers Thereof." Second Edition. London: A. R. Mowbray, 1963.

White, James F. *The Cambridge Movement: The Ecclesiologists and the Gothic Revival.* Cambridge: The University Press, 1963.

Woolley, Reginald Maxwell. *The Bread of the Eucharist.* Alcuin Club Tracts XI. London: A. R. Mowbray, 1913.